Positive Parenting for Autism

Powerful Strategies to Help Your Child Overcome Challenges and Thrive

VICTORIA M. BOONE, MA, BCBA

callisto
publishing
an imprint of Sourcebooks

Copyright © 2018 by Callisto Publishing LLC
Cover and internal design © 2018 by Callisto Publishing LLC
Cover photography: © Prostock-studio/Shutterstock; © MASTER PHOTO 2017/
Shutterstock; © Kenishirotie/Shutterstock
Interior Designer: Katy Brown
Cover Designer: Emma Hall
Editor: Camille Hayes
Production Editor: Erum Khan

Published by Callisto Publishing LLC C/O Sourcebooks LLC
P.O. Box 4410, Naperville, Illinois 60567-4410
(630) 961-3900
callistopublishing.com

Printed and bound in China
OGP 2

To my beautiful mother, Jeanmarie.

You said I could achieve anything I put my mind to, and you were right.

We dreamed of writing a book together, so this one is for you.

CONTENTS

INTRODUCTION

Throughout my years working as both a behavior therapist and a Board Certified Behavior Analyst (BCBA), I have met hundreds of family members, teachers, and special needs professionals in search of techniques to help them better support children with autism. For countless staff and caregivers, I have provided training and psychoeducation aimed at changing in a positive and lasting way the lives of the special needs children they worked with.

Raising a child with autism is one of the most challenging responsibilities any parent can face. When you are juggling work, family and social relationships, and outside commitments, it can be hard to manage life as a special needs parent and feel like you are doing all you can to support your child's growth and development. Parenting a child with autism can present a seemingly endless stream of problem behaviors to address, as well as special sensory and learning needs to consider, all while you're striving to teach your child the skills they need to thrive.

Each child with special needs is different, and so, too, are their caregivers' parenting goals. For some parents, the primary goal is for their first grader to say their first word; for others, the top priority could be to help their child learn to make eye contact and shake hands when meeting someone new. All parents want their kids to succeed and develop useful, adaptive skills and a sense of independence, but when your child has autism, helping them meet those goals can seem so challenging that you may not know where to start. The good news is there are powerful, scientifically proven techniques that can help your child with autism meet, and even exceed, the goals you envision for them. Applied behavior analysis (ABA), the gold-standard treatment for people with autism, can empower you to help your child develop essential life skills using positive, strengths-based strategies.

I wrote *Positive Parenting for Autism* because I want to put these powerful ABA tools—techniques I use every day in my professional life—directly into the hands of the people who need them most: parents and caregivers. Even if you're fortunate enough to have access to good supportive services in your community, you've no doubt learned that any progress your child makes in school or specialized programs can only be maintained if you continue their training at home. That's a tall order for many families, who might struggle to integrate their child's training protocol into their busy day-to-day lives. This book has been specifically designed not only to help you better understand your child's current training program, but also to teach you how to implement strategies tailored to your child's needs and goals at home.

This book provides concrete tools to help you develop personalized behavior change plans aimed at both increasing your child's positive behaviors and decreasing unwanted or problem behaviors. Each behavior change plan uses positive methods designed to build on your child's unique strengths, while teaching them essential adaptive behaviors and skills to reduce and remove problem behaviors. Each chapter walks you through a core ABA concept and provides plenty of examples of what the concept looks like in action. These examples are followed by specific techniques to help you create an individualized program designed to target the particular behaviors you seek to change in your child's life.

I hope *Positive Parenting for Autism* will be your guide as you support your child's ever-changing needs using these powerful, adaptable ABA techniques. With consistent work, you should start seeing noticeable results almost immediately. If you're anything like the parents I work with, you'll be amazed by the progress you see as your child learns, grows, and embarks on their path toward the bright future you want for them.

CHAPTER ONE

How to Use This Book

HOW IS THIS BOOK DIFFERENT?

As the number of autism diagnoses continues to increase worldwide, so does the need for effective interventions and useful resources. Many families I've worked with over the years have voiced frustration about how much time and effort it takes for them to get the services their children with autism need and deserve. In many cases, the services available where they live are limited to one or two providers, and they don't allow the kind of scheduling flexibility busy families need, adding logistical problems to the already challenging job of parenting a child with autism. On top of all that, these specialized services can be very costly for families if they're not covered by insurance or funded by local programs.

Now, more than ever, parents are looking for ways to implement or support their children's therapy at home, whether by reaching out to distant professionals via teleconferencing or other technology or, more often, buying resources to teach themselves about therapeutic techniques that will be helpful to their children.

Today, there are many autism books on the market; some focus on topics like understanding the diagnosis or learning to navigate the special education system, and many others are geared toward teaching parents and caregivers strategies to cope with the behavioral challenges they face at home. While such how-to books often contain very valuable information, they can be complicated, too technical, or just plain overwhelming for parents who are trying to balance the needs of their children with the many demands of work and home. Unfortunately, if a book is too difficult to get through, you will never see the full benefits of the strategies it aims to teach.

As a Board Certified Behavior Analyst (BCBA), I've spent years working with busy, concerned parents who are looking for ways to help their kids make healthy changes and get along better in life. They often struggle to make sense of competing advice they get from schools, health-care providers, and other specialists. I know parents want down-to-earth, practical advice on how to handle challenging behaviors and how to support and encourage their children in building on the strengths they already have. That's how this book came about: I wrote it in direct response to the struggles and challenges that parents like you have shared with me over the years.

Positive Parenting for Autism, like many books on autism, is based on applied behavior analysis (ABA), a proven-effective, scientifically based set of principles and strategies. However, unlike most books on ABA, this one is written just for you: a parent with a unique set of challenges and experiences; a parent of a child with autism. Alongside the ABA information, I've included real-life examples taken from my professional practice to help you understand how these new skills and strategies relate to the everyday situations you and your family face.

The thorough, practical guidance in *Positive Parenting for Autism* will help you feel confident about using these effective skill-building techniques to bring about positive, lasting change in your child's life. When you finish this book, you will have a solid foundation of the principles and clear, easy-to-use strategies you can readily implement at home. You can start using the tools in this book right away to develop your own in-home programs, bringing you one step closer to unlocking your child's full potential. These are the same evidence-based skills used by professionals everywhere, and they are guaranteed to get you results if you use them consistently and correctly.

WHAT IS APPLIED BEHAVIOR ANALYSIS?

Applied behavior analysis (ABA) is a science centered on strengthening positive, socially adaptive behavior by making changes to a person's immediate environment that *encourage* healthy behaviors and *discourage* problematic ones. By focusing on the events that occur right before and right after the behavior we want to change, we can determine what outcomes are more likely to reinforce the kind of behavior we want to see more of and what current actions may be supporting problematic behaviors.

ABA is unique in that it focuses on modifying events in the child's environment that will directly affect the behavior we seek to teach, increase, or decrease. I use ABA to improve the lives of my clients by focusing on what matters most—my clients' potential to live their most fulfilling lives. In general, ABA helps us understand *why* behaviors happen and gives us tools to systematically shape existing behavior, reduce maladaptive behavior, and teach new skills.

ABA first came to prominence in the mid-20th century, but its roots date back to the late 1800s with the birth of a branch of psychology now known as *behaviorism*. The father of behaviorism was psychologist John Watson. In Watson's time, psychology was dominated by researchers who focused only on the study of conscious and unconscious thought—in other words, the behind-the-scenes cognitive functions we can't see happening.

Watson founded the behaviorist movement by advocating for the study of observable human behavior—the things we do that other people can see, hear, or otherwise experience. This, Watson argued, was an equally important way to understand human psychology. In fact, Watson and other early behaviorists believed that everything could be explained solely by analyzing behavior. This outlook didn't change much until psychologist B. F. Skinner came along in the 1940s and argued for the inclusion of private events, what we call thoughts, in the study of human behavior. When Skinner shared his novel perspective on behavior with his colleagues in 1945, it was so unheard of that they actually called his idea radical. However, Skinner's radical behaviorism paved the way for the modern field of ABA, which uses the principles of human behavior that researchers uncovered to design interventions to help shape that behavior.

Today, ABA stands as the most effective treatment for individuals with autism, regardless of their age or level of functioning. Studies have shown that children who receive a minimum of 25 hours of ABA treatment per week develop more skills in less time than children who participate in other types of training. Now, this does not mean that you have to spend 25 hours a week implementing ABA techniques to see results. Any consistent use of these strategies will get you closer to the change you're working toward. Even a little goes a long way in ABA.

ABA continues to be a front-runner in autism treatment, in addition to being effective in addressing many other types of behavioral and psychological challenges. That's because ABA allows us to take a comprehensive look at people's behavior and environments and find infinitely adaptable ways to teach new skills in engaging and exciting ways.

HOW CAN ABA HELP YOU?

Successfully parenting a child with special needs is not easy. Your child may have difficulty focusing in school, engage in problem behaviors when there are changes in their routine, or need help with what can feel like simple tasks, such as communicating their needs to others or even getting dressed in the morning. These and many other challenges can easily lead you to feel stressed and overwhelmed.

You're not alone. Parents often struggle to find ways to ensure they're helping their children get their needs met while trying to help them develop adaptive skills that will afford them some level of independence. ABA is incredibly helpful in achieving this goal, because its tools will equip you to:

- Better understand why some of your child's behaviors are occurring
- Become more attuned to your child's needs and mode of communication
- Teach your child new and more effective methods of communication
- Teach your child adaptive living skills to help foster independence and connection (e.g., grooming and hygiene, coping skills, social skills, and requesting necessities)
- Encourage the development of prosocial behavior to help them connect to others
- Focus on reducing problematic behaviors while providing your child with positive, alternative behaviors that will work better for them

ABA is one of the most thoroughly researched and tested interventions available, and with it, you will have the information you need to start using techniques that have been helping kids with autism and other developmental challenges for more than 50 years.

ABA is also used by a wide array of professionals, even outside the treatment field. In fact, health and wellness coaches, human resource departments, teachers, sports professionals, and even casinos often use these techniques. For instance, a health and wellness coach would use ABA by creating a plan that modifies a client's environment and increases the likelihood of healthy behavior while decreasing instances of unhealthy behavior. One strategy might be to install a pull-up bar in the kitchen door-way—a simple environmental change that makes it easier to squeeze in a little exercise. When applied to the work environment, ABA principles are referred to as organizational behavior management (OBM). OBM strategies are used to enhance individual and group performance. These are just a few of the many ways that ABA is used to improve the world around us on a daily basis.

The adaptability of ABA and its principles to so many different scenarios means that once you learn and feel comfortable with these techniques, you can implement them to increase or decrease target behaviors across settings and people at whatever pace suits your needs. The beauty of this book is that it's focused on teaching you the same techniques that have been used by professionals in various fields for decades so that you, too, can successfully improve your life and the lives of those around you.

HOW DO I GET MY CHILD ON BOARD?

When I start working with a new family on ABA, the most common questions are "How can I get my child on board?" and "What happens if my child doesn't like this program?" Changes to any routine can be stressful, and they require focus and consistency to navigate smoothly. Whatever your child's level of functioning or temperament, my answer to getting a child on board is always the same: motivation.

With the right incentive, people can happily adapt to all sorts of things. Finding the right incentives is essential, because it will keep your child going through difficult moments and unwanted changes. To put it in perspective, think about how your performance at work would be affected if you knew you wouldn't receive a paycheck on a regular basis for your effort. Not only would your motivation drop, but so would your productivity and desire to participate in your boss's plan. Similarly, your child needs to be motivated and excited to get on board, especially with challenging things. With the correct motivators in place, this can be accomplished.

Generally, kids want to earn praise, have fun, and feel competent. As a parent, these three needs make up your holy grail—they are the keys to getting your child excited about starting and participating in your plan. Creating more opportunities for your child to be rewarded for positive behavior is part of any good behavior change plan. With ABA, you will teach your child that by engaging in certain behaviors, they will get the reinforcement they want, which creates the desire to engage in these appropriate behaviors and earn even more reinforcement. It may sound simple, but this cycle is incredibly powerful. I've seen kids so excited about the new competencies they're building that they ask what else they can do or how they can be more helpful to others. As a trainer, I find that to be an incredible feeling, and you may hear the same from your child when the right reinforcement is found.

ABA is all about increasing the "good stuff"—good behavior, opportunities for positive interactions, and reinforcement—and reducing the "not-so-good stuff"—problematic behavior, power struggles, and unhelpful communication. As a parent, you have the power not only to help your child improve, but also to create a program that will ensure they enjoy the process. Kids and adults alike thrive on positive reinforcement and feelings of accomplishment, and they will naturally engage in behaviors that increase their chances of receiving it—sometimes without even realizing that's what they're doing. Every time you catch your child being good and highlight their successes is an opportunity for them to see how much fun ABA can be.

Effective reinforcement is going to look different for each child. For some kids, imaginary play or listening to music are favorite activities, while other kids may prefer some special alone time. The most important thing to remember is that reinforcement should be as unique as your child. Keep exploring different options until you and your child have found what works to keep them motivated and focused on the work you're doing together. Also keep in mind that their preferences will change over time, so continue your exploration as you work toward your goals.

Parents often tell me that many of my sessions with their kids look more like play and praise than what they think of as "work," yet they still see tremendous improvement in their kids' behavior. The truth of the matter is that I *do* spend most of the time engaging in fun activities and delivering reinforcement. But what better way to get your child on board than by meeting them at their level, having fun with them, and praising them for every victory? By making ABA fun and motivating, you'll have your child practically begging for more "work." As with everything, practice makes perfect. ABA is such a veritable gold mine of helpful skills that implementing them may initially feel overwhelming. You don't need to try everything at once; this book simplifies the process for you and reminds you that your kid can do it, and so can you.

WHAT DO I NEED TO GET STARTED?

By reading this book, you've already moved one step closer to promoting positive change in your child's life. Each chapter breaks down a different concept or technique that will be invaluable in this behavior change process. To further support your new in-home ABA program, most of the chapters include a section called "Your Action Plan."

Each action plan will guide you through the necessary steps to create and launch a specific behavior change plan that incorporates the main ideas discussed in that chapter. After that, I'll walk you through how to create your intervention, organize your data sheet, and collect relevant data so you can put your newfound knowledge to use immediately. The sample data sheets included in the chapters give you an idea of how the process can look in action.

Before you begin, you'll need access to an analog or digital timer, as well as a large notebook and a pen or pencil so you have space to brainstorm intervention ideas and create your data collection sheets. You can also create data sheets in a word processing or spreadsheet program; you can print them out or record the information electronically. You'll find blank data sheets in the appendix (page 120), which you can photocopy if you'd like. However you decide to proceed, the most important thing is that you feel comfortable with the system you're using. When you have all that in place, you're ready to get started.

TAKEAWAYS

- The purpose of ABA is to improve socially significant behaviors by focusing on the environment around your child.
- ABA has remained one of the best—if not *the* best—available autism treatment interventions for more than 50 years.
- Understanding and applying ABA principles will help you identify targets for change and implement your own well-designed behavior change plans.
- By harnessing your child's motivation and desire for reinforcement, you create unlimited opportunities to foster your child's growth and enhance their quality of life.

CHAPTER TWO

What Is Your Child Telling You?

Using ABA to Decode Hidden Messages

WHEN BEHAVIOR SPEAKS LOUDER THAN WORDS

Communication is a fundamental necessity, because we need it to connect with others in a meaningful way. Without communication, we lose our sense of togetherness and the ability to express our needs and respond to the needs of others. There are more than seven billion people on this planet, with 6,500 languages spoken around the world, yet more than 93 percent of all human communication is nonverbal. The old saying, "Actions speak louder than words," is true in more ways than one. When you think about how much time we spend interacting with one another on a given day, it's amazing to think that most of our interactions happen without anyone saying a word.

Often, we get more input about the needs and motives of others from how they behave than we do from what they directly say to us. This can be

9

even more true for parents of children with limited verbal skills. It's important to remember that just because a child does not speak or engage in the kind of communication characteristic of neurotypical kids, it doesn't mean they don't have anything to say. Rather, they have the same needs and desires as the rest of us; they're just using different means to communicate to try to get those needs met. For many children with autism, there's only one avenue through which they're able to fully communicate: their behavior. That's one reason ABA is so helpful with these kids—it puts the focus on what they are doing and uses those behavior cues to determine how best to help them.

Just as importantly, ABA also provides us with tools that let us know if we are accidentally misinterpreting what a child is trying to tell us. For instance, when a toddler cries, there's a chance we might misinterpret the purpose of that cry. We may assume it's because he is hungry, when in reality, he may be tired or need to use the bathroom. Let's say we offer him a snack. If the crying continues, we can deduce that it is likely an attempt to communicate some other need or desire we haven't figured out yet. We might run through a series of options—"Are you thirsty?" "Do you want to lie down?"—before we find the correct answer through the process of elimination. If the toddler only stops crying after we take him to the restroom, we can safely deduce that he needed to relieve himself. Once we figure out which need the crying is meant to communicate, we can teach him a specific behavior, like the word *potty* or pointing to the bathroom, to signal his need in a more efficient way.

If your child is nonverbal, a hand signal might be the best way to communicate a need, at least in the beginning. But whether or not your child is verbal, the most important information you'll get from them will frequently be nonverbal—and that insight is the key to ABA's success as an intervention. ABA is like a decoder key that will help you decipher the hidden messages behind your child's behaviors by providing you with tools to figure out the true motives behind those behaviors. In the same way you'll decipher messages by analyzing your child's behavior, you can alter the environment to create messages that will guide your child toward more adaptive, prosocial behaviors.

Detective Work

The role of a detective is to do the investigative work necessary to solve a mystery. They do this by collecting relevant information, searching old records or databases, and making objective observations. In the same way, you are the detective, and your goal is to collect enough evidence based on information and observations to solve the behavioral mystery in front of you.

One way to do this is by being cognizant of what is going on around your child when they engage in different behaviors. For example, if your child starts having a tantrum every time you tell them it is bath time, it is likely that they are trying to communicate that they don't want to take a bath, perhaps because the lighting in the bathroom is too bright or they don't like the water temperature. In this scenario, your previous data on tantrums and your current observations can help you solve the mystery. Similarly, if your child yawns and acts sleepy when it's time to do the dishes or clean their room, you can deduce that their excessive yawning behavior is an attempt to avoid having to complete their chores.

Whether your goal is to increase prosocial behavior, decrease maladaptive behavior, or build new skills in your child's repertoire, knowing the "why" and "how" behind your child's current behaviors and those you want to see helps you plan for and reach the behavior change goals you desire. ABA professionals do this by conducting a functional behavior assessment (FBA).

An FBA is an analytical process based on observation that helps us determine the function (or purpose) of behavior, brainstorm ways to more appropriately meet that function, and determine how changes in the environment can be made to better support the desired behavior change. The FBA helps ABA professionals do a lot of our detective work, because it involves the compilation of information from multiple people in the child's life when possible, as well as the parents' observations of the child's current behavior patterns. In short, we make note of what behaviors (both positive and negative) the child engages in, along with the events that occur before, during, and after these behaviors.

By closely looking at possible behavior trends or patterns, you are one step closer to decoding the hidden messages your child is sending and to finding ways to improve their ability to communicate those messages to you. The foundation of a successful FBA relies on your ability to recognize the ABCs—the three components of behavior change. In the next section, I'll break down these components so you can better understand how to assess the reason behind each behavior and ultimately decide how to best approach your behavior change plan.

LEARNING YOUR ABCs

To truly understand how ABA works, you must start by learning your ABCs. The ABCs of behavior analysis are almost as easy to learn as the alphabet, and—in my opinion—they are just as fundamental. *ABC* stands for "antecedent," "behavior," and "consequence," which together form the building blocks of any successful behavior change program. Once you understand them, you're well on your way to mastering the "why" and "how" of behavior change. I'll start by breaking down the definition of each ABC term, and then we'll explore an example to better illustrate the concepts.

The antecedent, or *A*, is anything that happens right before the behavior you're interested in changing. The antecedent can give you some insight into which things in your child's environment—circumstances or events—may signal that you're likely to see a particular behavior. The behavior itself, or *B*, can be anything your child says or does after the antecedent. The consequence, or *C,* is what occurs after the behavior, and it can have the effect of either increasing or decreasing the likelihood that the behavior will happen again.

We commonly associate the word *consequence* with punishment—as in, "There will be consequences if you misbehave, young man!" But, in ABA, a consequence can be either positive or negative—like getting a bonus at work for increased productivity or getting a ticket for speeding. A consequence must occur after a behavior and have some effect on it. The most important thing to remember about consequences is that they determine whether the behavior will increase or decrease in the future. They are the reinforcers, and sometimes the "punishers," that either increase or decrease a given behavior.

To demonstrate how the ABCs are used, I like to use a headache analogy. Usually, when we start to feel a headache coming on, most of us will take some form of pain reliever, hoping the headache subsides once the medication starts working. The *antecedent* in this scenario is the onset of the headache—the pain we feel. In response to the pain, we take the medication—that's the *behavior*. The ideal *consequence* would no more headache, but let's analyze both possible outcomes in this scenario. If the consequence is alleviating the headache after taking the medication, we'll be more likely to take it in the future because we know it works. In that case, we'd say taking the medication was *reinforced*. If the consequence had been the reverse—the headache lingered or got worse—we would be a lot less likely to take that medication in the future. In that case, taking the medication would be *punished* with continued or more pain. As you can see, the ABCs shape our behavior even with something as simple as a headache!

We'll explore reinforcement and punishment more in later chapters, but for now, just remember that these are the two main possible consequences in the ABCs. Once you've got this down, you're one step closer to embarking on this behavior change journey to improve your child's life and daily functioning.

Now that you know about antecedents, behaviors, and consequences, you are ready to conduct your own FBA on an ABC data sheet, like this:

Sample ABC Data Sheet

TIME	ANTECEDENT	BEHAVIOR	CONSEQUENCE	POSSIBLE FUNCTION (OR PURPOSE)

The first step in collecting ABC data is to set aside uninterrupted time during which you can observe and take notes on your child's behavior. Whenever the behavior happens, the first thing you'll do is write the time it happened in the Time column and the exact actions your child engaged in under the Behavior column.

Next, you will write down what happened before the behavior in the Antecedent column and what occurred after the behavior in the Consequence column. As you continue to fill in this information about the behavior every time it happens, you may begin to notice patterns. For example, a behavior may always occur right after someone else is being given attention or once something preferred is taken away. These patterns will give you clues that can better explain why these behaviors are happening in the first place, which you will record in the last column.

The ABCs in Action: Hannah's Story

Seven-year-old Hannah's mother was worried about her daughter's problematic "haircutting" behavior. Because Hannah had limited verbal skills, her mother was left guessing why Hannah continued to chop off her own hair. During our intake appointment, Hannah's mother told me that no matter how many times they attempted to tie Hannah's hair up or keep it off her face, she would always find strands of hair to cut off when no one was looking. Although she had taken Hannah to get a haircut, hoping that if it was shorter and out of her way, she would leave it alone, Hannah continued to find ways to cut strands of hair, even if the hair belonged to her dolls.

After two weeks of trying to figure out why Hannah was so determined to cut hair, I started to worry it would remain an unsolved mystery . . . until I went to their home and started collecting data on what I observed just before and just after Hannah's haircutting occurred. I began recording ABC data to take a closer look at what events in her environment might explain this behavior. By the third day of data collection, I noticed that Hannah would cut hair when her mother was engaged in activities that diverted her attention away from Hannah.

In one instance, Hannah's mother was on the phone with a friend and hung up in shock when she realized that Hannah had found the scissors and had started cutting her hair again. The consequence of Hanna's haircutting was that her mom ended her phone call and started paying attention to Hannah. The second time, her mother was doing the dishes and stopped immediately to put the scissors away when she turned around to find that Hannah was at it again. By the third day, it was clear that Hannah's haircutting behavior was being reinforced by the attention she was getting from her mother every time she caught her at it.

Now, typically, when a behavior is being maintained by attention, we devise a plan in which we ignore the inappropriate attention-seeking behavior so that it no longer serves that purpose. But because the attention-seeking behavior in this scenario involved the use of scissors, I decided it was not safe to simply ignore Hannah. Instead, we used a three-part intervention to decrease her problematic behavior while teaching Hannah more socially appropriate ways to get her mom's attention.

The first part involved removing all scissors and potential haircutting items from the home to eliminate the possibility of haircutting. We also increased the length of time Hannah and her mom regularly spent together, assuming that if Hannah got lots of attention and social praise from her mom, she'd be less likely to seek it out when her mother was busy with other things. Last, we taught Hannah that to gain attention from her mom or other care-givers, she had to raise her hand, tap them on the shoulder, or say, "Excuse me." We continued this intervention over the next month and slowly reintroduced the presence of scissors while still reinforcing Hannah's appropriate attention-seeking behavior by giving her the requested attention when she asked the right way. Our plan was a huge success. Once we used the ABCs to understand the reason behind Hannah's behavior, we could focus our attention on finding new ways to meet the needs her behavior was expressing.

MEASURING YOUR OUTCOMES

As you work your way through this book and begin creating your own set of behavior change programs, you'll want to monitor your progress. Monitoring progress lets you know how close you are to your goal and gives you enough information to make an informed decision when your plan may not be working. If this happens, do not get discouraged. Even as a professional, I make it a priority to regularly examine a child's progress to determine if the intervention plan is the best fit for this particular learner, or if something needs to be changed for them to be more successful. This is the foundation of my profession and the core of your own program's success.

It is extremely important to keep ongoing records by collecting data, as mentioned earlier. Keeping records allows you to continually see what is and isn't working. It's also a wonderful source of information in determining what direction you would like to move in next. Sometimes it can be difficult to understand what your child needs to be successful, unless you have a plan and system for information collection in place.

To illustrate: Once, I was teaching a client how to shower independently. We had been working on showering for three or four months; I would verbally go through the steps with her and also prompt her during actual showers. I believed she was more independent than she presented, but she still needed a lot of prompting. As it turned out, her mom was still prompting too much, which made her daughter prompt dependent. I made a deal with her mom: We could start working on a different goal if she spent a week collecting her own data on her daughter's independent showering routine. She eagerly agreed. After a week of collecting data, my client's mom could not believe how much less support her daughter needed. She expressed how helpful it was for her to collect her own data, because it allowed her to identify specific steps her daughter was missing, as well as those her daughter could do on her own, giving her a more targeted approach when she focused on her daughter's showering outside of the sessions. Within a week, her daughter was showering by herself!

Creating a plan and collecting her own data gave this mother goals to focus on and a clear path to success. It is amazing how powerful a tool data collection can be. In each subsequent chapter, I will help you create tracking sheets for each action plan so you can track your child's progress toward each goal.

CREATING THE BEST PROGRAM FOR YOUR CHILD

Your child's skill sets, individual needs, and behaviors are different from other children's. In fact, the only thing that is identical across all individuals with autism spectrum disorder is the *name* of the diagnosis. Aside from this, no two people with any of these diagnoses are the same.

Every child is special and possesses unique characteristics that are significant to their identity and their interactions with the world around them. It is for this reason that each child requires an individualized behavior change program that will best meet their needs while taking into account their individual strengths and weaknesses. Therefore, no two ABA programs are the same. Each one will seek to maximize the child's strengths, provide additional support in areas that need improvement, build and maintain adaptive life skills, and reduce problem behaviors. Your ABA program will target these goals in a unique way that meets your child wherever they are developmentally. When you create a plan that uniquely addresses your child's needs while considering their areas of relative strength, you will set your child up for success and increase their probability of personal growth and capability.

The beauty of ABA lies in its applicability to a wide range of settings and people, as well as the versatility with which each strategy can be implemented to suit your needs. One parent's ABA program may focus on teaching their child to appropriately make requests for items or activities, tie their shoes, and get dressed independently. Another parent's goals may be to reduce the frequency of their child's problem behavior, help them implement better coping skills, and develop more independent living or vocational skills. Regardless of your goal for your child's ABA journey, the fundamental skills you use remain the same. The way you choose to implement the skills to reach the goals you set for your child is what will be different.

When it comes to your child, you are the most knowledgeable expert; you understand their needs and areas for growth in ways others cannot. You are more aware than anyone else of your child's adaptive skills, their common routines and behavior patterns, their difficulties in communication or interaction, and their problem behaviors. Therefore, your role as a parent is the most important one within the ABA treatment process. As the parent, you can not only create the best plan of practice for you and your family, but also teach other professionals and caregivers who work with your child how to support your new behavior change plan. When you effectively communicate your ABA program and give important feedback or tips for success, you are ensuring that your child is practicing these skills across settings and people. This increases the likelihood that these positive changes will remain.

TAKEAWAYS

- Your detective work is critical in solving the mystery behind the "why" of your child's actions and helping create a cohesive plan of action.
- You serve as your child's expert and have the opportunity to teach them skills that will drastically improve their quality of life.
- Determine the function (or purpose) of your child's behavior to assess their need, and then develop alternative ways to help them communicate that need effectively.
- Take the time to analyze the antecedents and consequences that are maintaining the behavior of concern, and, with this information, create an effective plan geared toward positive behavior change.

CHAPTER THREE

Choosing the Power of Reinforcement

WHAT IS REINFORCEMENT?

A *reinforcer* is anything that comes after the occurrence of a behavior and increases the likelihood that the behavior will happen again in the future. In other words, it is a type of consequence that helps a behavior increase. Think of reinforcement as functioning somewhat like rewards. When you reward your child with ice cream after they clean their room, it's because you like the room-cleaning behavior and want to see more of it. That's how reinforcement works, and when you use it mindfully, it's with the express purpose of increasing the frequency of behaviors you like. (Parents can also sometimes accidentally reinforce behaviors they're trying to get rid of, but more on that later.)

Reinforcement is the foundation of any effective behavior change program, and the success of reinforcement, as a strategy, relies heavily on the effectiveness of the reinforcers you use. For instance, paying your teen an allowance once they complete their chores could be considered reinforcement if the allowance motivates them to get their chores done. Another example could be letting a younger child have 20 extra minutes of TV time, because they ate all of their vegetables at dinner. In each case, the reinforcer is matched to the child's motivations, partly based on their age group.

Reinforcement is a uniquely valuable tool for parents, because it can be used to teach a wide array of different behaviors, from learning to use utensils properly to learning how to drive a car. Reinforcement can be used to help you address many or most of the challenges you'll encounter while parenting your child with autism. Reinforcement is also special in that it teaches kids new behavior—and modifies their existing behavior—in a way that is positive and strengths based.

With reinforcement, you spend most of your time rewarding your child for what they're doing *right*—rather than correcting or punishing the things that go wrong. In a reinforcement-based program, your child gets lots of opportunities to recognize their own growth and feel proud of themselves, track their own progress, and receive plenty of encouragement along the way to their goals. Studies have shown that children who regularly receive reinforcement show a 10 percent increase in the size of their hippocampus—the part of the brain that helps with emotional regulation, learning, and memory formation (Luby et al. 2016). Your words and actions literally have an effect on your child's emotional and intellectual growth.

In the next section, I'll break down the different types of reinforcement and illustrate how each can be used to improve your child's behavior.

Positive versus Negative Reinforcement

The two types of reinforcement are *positive* and *negative*. When applied to the reinforcement process, those words have a slightly different meaning than you might be used to. Here, *positive* and *negative* don't mean "good" and "bad." Both positive and negative reinforcement will lead to an increase in future occurrences of the reinforced behavior. In this instance, it's better to think of the positive/negative distinction in terms of *addition* versus *subtraction*—that is, does the reinforcement involve adding something to the child's environment (positive reinforcement) or removing something from it (negative reinforcement)?

POSITIVE REINFORCEMENT

Let's look first at the definition of positive reinforcement. *Positive reinforcement* is the immediate addition of a stimulus that, when it is made contingent on a behavior, increases the future frequency of that behavior. When you're using positive reinforcement, a behavior occurs and is then followed by something desirable that will encourage the behavior to happen again in the future. An example of this could be a high five; saying, "Nice job"; or awarding points, strategies similar to what teachers use with students to reinforce good behavior throughout the day.

Let's say your child struggles with changes in their daily routine. In this example, their normal babysitter is sick, so your child has a different babysitter that day. This can be a very dramatic transition, which might result in more problem behaviors like whining or not following directions they normally comply with. Reinforcement could be used by delivering a desired treat or form of social praise each time your child listens to the new babysitter without engaging in those problem behaviors. Or let's say your child has a hard time cooperating when it is time to put away their tablet. This would be an opportunity to provide positive reinforcers, maybe in the form of an extra scoop of ice cream for dessert for good behavior when tablet time is up.

Positive reinforcement is a powerful tool for encouraging and shaping healthy, adaptive behavior. However, if you're not careful, you can also inadvertently reinforce undesirable behavior. Let's take a look at another example: Your child asks you for the tablet to play games, and you say no. If your child is the stubborn type, this could result in their repeatedly asking to use it and even following you around whining, hoping you'll change your mind. Some parents have told me that they often give in at that point, because sometimes it's easier to do that, especially if the parent is tired or has other things to do.

But think about what the child is learning in that situation. What behavior is being reinforced? By giving them the tablet after they whine or ask repeatedly, the parent is teaching their child two things: The first is that if they engage in maladaptive behavior for long enough, they will get what they want. The second is that they don't have to take their parent at their word, because, with enough persistence, a *no* becomes a *yes*. The result is that, because it worked in the past, the child is more likely to engage in similar, if not more intense, whining and demanding behavior in the future. As difficult as it may be, the parent in this scenario should continue to withhold access to the tablet to ensure they follow through on their *no* and don't accidentally reinforce their child's unpleasant behavior.

Reinforcers are different for everyone. When choosing reinforcers for your child, keep in mind that what one child finds desirable (and is therefore reinforcing)—say, lemonade—another child might find undesirable (and is therefore is not reinforcing). Likewise, something *you* assume to be fun may actually be aversive to your child or not motivating enough for them to engage in the desired behavior. For instance, I once worked with a child who would cry whenever someone offered her a high five or said, "Great job." I soon discovered that this child preferred a silent nod or fist bump when she engaged in appropriate behavior. I knew this was a reinforcer for her, because it led to an increase in the frequency and intensity of her desirable behaviors.

Some parents have told me that nothing is an effective reinforcer for their child; they've tried everything, and nothing worked. I remind them that a reinforcer is something that makes the frequency of the behavior increase. If the behavior does not increase, then by definition, what those parents are using are not really reinforcers. It is up to you to work with your child to determine what things or events are most reinforcing. The best way to figure this out may be to ask your child or give them different options and have them choose. You can also observe your child during their free time to see what they gravitate toward, and add those items or activities to your list of reinforcers. Sometimes you'll have to be creative with your discovery of reinforcers. This could mean deciding if some of your child's unique interests, such as repetitive play with toy cars or even asking for "squeezes," can be used as reinforcers.

NEGATIVE REINFORCEMENT

Let's turn now to negative reinforcement. People who are unfamiliar with the language of ABA often mistake negative reinforcement for punishment, because the word *negative* has such a familiar, adverse connotation. But remember, reinforcement is anything that results in an increase of the behavior that's being reinforced. So whether it's positive or negative reinforcement, by definition, it's an outcome the child desires.

Negative reinforcement is the immediate contingent removal of a stimulus that *increases* the likelihood the behavior will occur again. When I say "contingent," I mean that the removal of the stimulus is solely dependent upon whether the target behavior happens. This means that when a behavior happens, the contingent consequence will be the removal of something unpleasant, which will cause the target behavior to increase. If the behavior does not happen, then the stimulus is not removed. Here's an example:

telling your child that if they take a bite of one new food that they have never tried, they don't have to finish the veggies on their plate.

The important thing to keep in mind with negative reinforcement is that the goal, from the child's perspective, is always to escape or avoid something they don't like—what is called a "non-preferred" thing or event. That's the "negative" part—you are *removing* the undesired thing (chores) from the child's environment to reinforce doing homework. If your kid hates doing dishes, they will probably do their homework as requested to avoid that chore. This illustrates negative reinforcement, because homework completion (the behavior) will be followed by the removal of chores (the consequence). In the future, your child will probably be more likely to complete their homework if they know it will result in the removal of a chore.

Because reinforcement is so powerful, it's important to use it mindfully so you aren't inadvertently reinforcing behaviors you're trying to eliminate. This phenomenon is more common than you might think. Now, let's look at an example where maladaptive behaviors are accidentally strengthened by way of negative reinforcement.

Say your child is presented with homework, and again, you tell them they can skip chores if they finish their homework. Even if chores are aversive, if they dislike doing homework so much that getting out of chores is not a strong enough reinforcer, they may respond by yelling, pushing, or engaging in similar problematic behaviors. Perhaps, like many parents, you respond to outbursts like that by sending your child to their room, thinking that doing so is a form of punishment. What actually happens, however, is that your child has escaped from homework altogether, which was the original request you made. By yelling and pushing, they got to go to their room and escape doing both homework *and* chores—so the yelling and pushing are inadvertently being reinforced. Your child has now learned that maladaptive behavior helps them avoid unpleasant situations, and you can guarantee that the next time they're asked to do something they don't like, you'll see the undesirable behavior again.

As you work with your child, it's important to remember that negative reinforcement could result in the increase of maladaptive behavior if it is not used correctly. By determining the function, or purpose, of the behavior, as discussed in chapter 2, you'll understand whether it should be reinforced or not. For instance, the function of the child's maladaptive behavior in the previous example was avoidance of non-preferred activities. By allowing the child to escape from homework and chores, the parent negatively reinforced the yelling and pushing behaviors. A better response would be to make sure the child still completes the homework despite the tantrum.

Regardless of which reinforcers you use, be sure to only give them to your child when they engage in the desired behavior you're targeting. If they have access to the reinforcer, when they are not doing what you've asked, it will not be an effective reinforcer because they can get it without having to earn it.

Reinforcement affects your ability to teach and change your child's behavior, but the amazing thing about reinforcement is that it plays an integral role in the social and occupational functioning of *everyone* on a daily basis. The following section highlights how reinforcement presents itself in our lives on a regular basis, even when it isn't obvious.

REINFORCEMENT IS ALL AROUND YOU

Reinforcement is responsible for most of the behaviors we engage in—we all respond to reinforcers, both positive and negative.

Once you look for it, you'll see that many everyday behaviors are maintained through the process of negative reinforcement. For example, if you're driving without your seat belt, you will likely hear an annoying chime reminding you to fasten it. The antecedent in this scenario is the annoying chime you hear, and the behavior is your fastening your seat belt. The consequence is that the chime stops, and in the future, you're more likely to once again fasten your seat belt to avoid hearing the unpleasant noise. That's negative reinforcement: Something undesirable has been removed. Another example of this is scratching an itch. Feeling the itch is the antecedent that triggers the scratching behavior. The consequence of scratching is that the uncomfortable itch sensation is alleviated, which reinforces your scratching behavior.

Now let's look at positive reinforcement. Earning a paycheck is the most common example. The need to pay bills and maintain a standard of living is the antecedent that causes you to go to work for a certain amount of time each week. The behavior of going to work means you will get paid for your time, so in this situation, your earned paycheck is the consequence—the reinforcer. If you went to work but did not earn a paycheck or other benefits, the chances you would continue to work would no doubt decrease quite a bit.

As you can see, most of the reinforcement in our lives occurs naturally, and we seldom realize it's happening. People, on the whole, tend to respond better and learn better from reinforcement than from punishment. That's largely because reinforcement results in our either gaining something we want or escaping something we dislike—positive environmental events that leave our brains open and primed for learning. One of the drawbacks of punishment is that the delivery of something aversive—like yelling or taking away your child's favorite toy—is stressful. As I'm sure you know, when we're stressed out, we don't learn as quickly or as well. That means the learning that happens under punishment conditions is suboptimal.

The Difference Between Reinforcement and "Bribery"

In many ways, reinforcement is the most powerful tool at your disposal, but some parents still resist the idea of consistently rewarding good behavior, because it reminds them of bribery. But if you're doing it correctly, reinforcement is nothing like bribery. Let's examine the key differences between the two.

One notable difference is the timing of the reinforcer delivery. Reinforcement is set up in advance; with reinforcement, the "ground rules" are laid out ahead of time, and the reward comes only after the target behavior has taken place. Bribery, on the other hand, happens when you offer a preferred stimulus in the *middle* of a problem behavior to make it go away. You give the child what they want first, based on their promise to engage in the desired behavior, and the prize is being offered after an undesirable behavior is already happening.

Bribery is a source of negative reinforcement for you, because bribing your child allows *you* to escape the aversive situation at hand. In other words, bribery is meant to benefit the person who is delivering the bribe, while reinforcement benefits the child by teaching them that they have to *earn* the consequence and can only do so by engaging in appropriate behavior. By definition, reinforcement means that the appropriate behavior will increase in the future. This is not true of bribery, because it temporarily changes the present situation to benefit the bribe-giver, but it does not teach the child new appropriate skills to implement in future situations.

Another difference between reinforcement and bribery is the language used. Bribery sounds like, "I'll give you [prize] if you do [task]," whereas reinforcement sounds like, "If you do [task], then you can *earn* [prize]." Here's an example of a bribe: Your child does not want to transition from snack time to homework time, so they start whining and having a tantrum. While this is going on, you say, "If you get up and stop whining, I will give you two lollipops." Your child promises to stop whining and sits down at the desk, and you hand over the lollipops. As soon as they are done with the lollipops and you say it's time to start homework, they start the problem behaviors all over again.

Bribery will work in the short term; however, it also teaches your child to wait for the bribe, because they know you will give it to them. Instead of your child learning the skill you are trying to teach, they learn *you* can be controlled long enough to give them a bribe. By understanding the power and prevalence of reinforcement, you can learn to use it skillfully and effectively to create positive change for yourself and your child without worrying that you are resorting to bribery.

YOUR ACTION PLAN

Now that you have a better understanding of how to use reinforcement, let's apply what you've learned by giving you the opportunity to use reinforcement to change your child's behavior. The first step is to pick a behavior you want to teach or modify. Your behavior goal should be objective, simple, and measurable, and it should include positive language. In other words, frame it in terms of what your child *should* do rather than what they *shouldn't* do.

Here's an example of positive language: "Valeria will finish 10 math problems within five consecutive minutes." In contrast, here's an example of negative framing: "Allyson will stop whining during homework time every night." The first example uses positive language by highlighting the desired behavior instead of focusing on the behavior Valeria's parent wants to decrease. The positive language is also more objective and measurable, because the focus is on five consecutive minutes instead of general homework time. The parent knows that Valeria has to finish 10 math problems specifically during the five-minute period.

Defining a goal this way makes it easier for multiple caregivers to provide reinforcement, because everyone will be on the same page with regard to what the desired behavior is. It also gives your child a positive goal to work toward, instead of a negative behavior to run from. Make sure your goal is something that can be measured quickly, does not span a lengthy amount of time, and is attainable for your child. Remember, you can always adjust goals as your child reaches or surpasses them.

Reinforcement in Action: Ella's Story

I started seeing Ella shortly after she was diagnosed with autism at around age three. When she came to me, she was nonverbal and had difficulty engaging with peers. After six months of intervention, she'd said her first words and started having weekly playdates where she was learning to engage in age-appropriate play and was actually making friends.

After a year of services, Ella had improved tremendously and often received compliments from friends and family about how brilliant and articulate she was. She enjoyed playing "teacher" and sharing information with her parents and classmates, or, as Ella would call them, her "new students." Once Ella had reached all her goals, we decided she was in a great place and faded out services.

A year later, I got a call from Ella's parents, because they were concerned that her language skills were regressing after the birth of her younger brother nine months earlier. She had started using baby talk to communicate and would whine or make babbling noises when greeting adults. Ella's teacher also reported that she had begun to recite the morning ABCs and sight words in that same manner and was no longer engaging in age-appropriate activities with her peers, only wanting to play with them if they pretended to act and talk like babies or treated her like one. After speaking with Ella's parents, it was clear that Ella's speech likely started regressing after seeing how much attention her baby brother was getting when he attempted to speak.

Rather than reprimanding Ella or commenting on her maladaptive talking behavior, I focused on using positive reinforcement to increase her age-appropriate talking behavior. Every time she spoke without using baby talk (even if all she said was hello), we would deliver her favorite reinforcers—high fives and tickles—and say, "Wow! I love when you use your big girl voice." After four days, Ella's parents were thrilled to let me know Ella was no longer using baby talk. In fact, she was having more than double the number of age-appropriate conversations than before she'd started using baby talk. During my next home visit, I even saw Ella trying to teach her brother how to "talk like a big kid." Cheers to the power of reinforcement!

For the next step in your plan, you'll need to decide how often you will reinforce the target behavior: Every time you see it? Every time a set period elapses? Deciding how often you will reinforce a behavior is a *schedule of reinforcement*. Schedules of reinforcement allow you to control the timing and frequency of your reinforcers.

An *interval schedule of reinforcement* means that you will base your reinforcement delivery on whether the desired behavior happens within a specified time interval. For instance, if your child's schedule of reinforcement for solving math problems is two minutes, you would deliver a reinforcer after they have completed a math problem within that two-minute period. If you were to use a *ratio schedule of reinforcement*, the reinforcer delivery would depend on the number of correct responses. To illustrate, let's say your child's schedule of reinforcement is now every five correct responses. That means they have to answer five math problems correctly, regardless of how much time passes, to get the reinforcer.

Generate a list of effective reinforcers so you have plenty to choose from once your behavior change plan gets off the ground. Start by making a list of your child's favorite foods, drinks, games, activities, and forms of social praise (e.g., hugs, tickles, high fives, positive statements, etc.). This list should also include unique interests, daily activities, and privileges your child currently has access to that can be used as reinforcers. This gives you a comprehensive list of things you can use as you're testing your new reinforcement skills. Remember, this list will likely change frequently, and that is okay. Don't be afraid to introduce your child to new items or activities to give them an opportunity to develop new reinforcers.

When you first begin working on a goal, the best way to increase the behavior is by reinforcing every instance of it immediately after it occurs, and then decreasing the amount of reinforcement over time once your child has fully acquired the skill. That would mean that if your child finishes 10 math problems within five minutes, they should gain immediate access to the reinforcer. Since the goal for your child, in this example, is to continue working on math problems, you might be concerned that delivering a reinforcer every five minutes will interrupt the math homework. In this case, it might be ideal to give your child a token or point after each five-minute increment that can be traded in for a reinforcer at the end of homework time.

If you decide to use the token system, the reinforcer and its token price must be preestablished. This way, your child knows what they are working toward and what they have to do to get it before the activity even begins. The reinforcer should also be paired with an acknowledgment that highlights why they are receiving it so your child understands that their target behavior is the reason they are earning the reinforcer. The praise should always be specific and emphasize your recognition of their new behavior.

TAKING YOUR MEASUREMENTS

Let's go through the steps you'll need to take to start collecting your data. In the sample data sheet to follow, you will see how all of this plays out, using Valeria as an example. Valeria is working for five minutes of outside play and five minutes of computer time. The reinforcer is effective if Valeria continues to complete 10 math problems during each of the five-minute intervals to gain access to the play time.

1. Always let your child know what they are earning for the behavior before you start so they remain motivated to work toward it. You can also alternate between different reinforcers and measure whether the behavior increases with certain reinforcers.

2. Use a reinforcement data sheet, such as the one on page 30, to help you track your progress. The data sheet should be easy to read and fill in so you and other caregivers can do so quickly. Setting up the data sheet in a table format will likely be the best way to capture all the information you need. In the top row of the data sheet, include five headings: Date, Time, Target Behavior, Reinforcer Used, and Yes/No. In each of the subsequent rows, you'll have room to record your data. Under the Time column, fill in the time intervals during which you will be collecting data.

3. Keep the data sheet and list of reinforcers in an easily accessible location. For instance, if your child is doing homework at the dining room table but the data sheet and list of reinforcers are in the car, the chances of taking accurate data and delivering reinforcers in a timely manner will decrease.

4. Measure behavior across at least five different time intervals to see if it is truly effective. You can even collect data across multiple days.

When you have taken these steps, your final product will probably look something like the sample sheet on page 30.

Sample Reinforcement Data Sheet

DATE	TIME	TARGET BEHAVIOR	REINFORCER USED	YES/NO
5/4	5:15–5:20 pm	Working on math quietly	5 min. of outside play	No
5/4	5:20–5:25 pm	Working on math quietly	5 min. of computer time	Yes
5/5	5:45–5:50 pm	Working on math quietly	5 min. of outside play	No
5/6	4:15–4:20 pm	Working on math quietly	5 min. of computer time	Yes
5/6	5:15–5:20 pm	Working on math quietly	5 min. of computer time	Yes

Since we know a reinforcer, by definition, is anything that makes a behavior increase, by looking at the sheet, we can deduce that outside play is not a reinforcer for Valeria, but computer time is. Valeria's parents or other caregivers would therefore continue to use computer time and other effective reinforcers to maintain Valeria's homework behavior.

TAKEAWAYS

- Reinforcement is one of the building blocks of behavior change.
- Nearly all of our interactions with others and daily activities are guided by our innate response to the reinforcers in our environment.
- Negative reinforcement allows us to avoid or escape from unwanted tasks or activities by engaging in a specific behavior, while positive reinforcement means we acquire access to a task or activity also by way of a specific behavior.
- By using a strengths-based strategy like reinforcement to effect change in the life of your child, you are able to maximize their potential for growth and learning while boosting their self-confidence.

CHAPTER FOUR

What Is Punishment, and Should You Use It?

WHAT IS PUNISHMENT?

In chapter 3, you learned that reinforcement occurs when a behavior is followed by an event that increases the likelihood it will occur again in the future. Punishment is the exact opposite of reinforcement; it's the procedure we use when we want to *decrease* the likelihood we'll see a behavior again.

Reinforcement and punishment are both forms of learning, and in some scenarios, punishment can be the more efficient means of helping us *quickly* learn to avoid situations that could pose an immediate danger. For example, let's say you've never seen a hot stove before and you decide to touch it. The pain of the burn you'd likely receive would be aversive enough that you'd be deterred from repeating the same behavior in the future. Although painful, the punishment would serve as a powerful learning experience that would keep you safe in similar situations in the future.

In a more common example, let's say your child forgets to do their homework, so as a consequence, their teacher doesn't let them go to recess that day. If the denial of recess is unpleasant enough, then in the future, your child will make sure the day's homework is done to avoid missing recess again. Another example, common to adults, is late fees on a forgotten bill. That extra charge is usually financially painful enough to cause us to keep closer track of our billing statements so it doesn't happen again. This kind of targeted, careful application of punishment is found in many places in our environments. When properly used, punishment doesn't carry such strong aversive consequences that it creates unintended negative outcomes. However, when using punishment, you should always be aware of the possibility of misuse, and do what you can to safeguard against it.

Before we focus on when and how to best use punishment, let's look more closely at the different types of punishment.

Positive versus Negative Punishment

Any type of punishment will lead to a decrease in the behavior that's being punished. But like reinforcement, punishment comes in two main types: positive and negative. If the idea of positive punishment sounds strange, remember that in ABA, *positive* and *negative* don't mean "good" and "bad." Instead, positive refers to the addition of a stimulus to the environment, and negative refers to stimulus removal.

So, *positive punishment* is the addition of something immediately following a behavior, which leads to a decrease in that behavior in the future. A late fee on a forgotten bill is an example of positive punishment—the *addition* of the late fee causes a decrease in the late-bill-paying behavior. An example of *negative punishment* would be the common parenting tactic of taking away a kid's favorite item—say, an electronic device—when the child misbehaves. The parent assumes that the removal of the desired object, when made contingent on the disruptive behavior, will reduce the frequency of that behavior in the future.

TYPES OF POSITIVE PUNISHMENT

Let's take a moment here to look at examples of different types of positive punishment, because this punishment is the easiest to misuse and should be handled with care and awareness. In the world of ABA, there are five common types of positive punishment, as follows:

Verbal reprimand: This is a reprimand or any verbal warning used to express disappointment or disapproval. An example of this is telling your child to "stop playing with that toy and focus on your work" when you see them getting distracted instead of finishing their school project.

Overcorrection: This means restoring the environment to a condition that is better than when you started the undesirable behavior. For example, your child is supposed to put their clean clothes away, but you catch them pushing the clothes under the bed to avoid the work. As a punishment, not only does your child have to put their clean clothes away, but now they also have to clean the rest of their room, too.

Positive practice: This means repeatedly engaging in an appropriate replacement for the undesirable behavior, either for a certain number of times or for a specific duration. For example, your child runs across the parking lot to your parked car without looking out for cars. You bring your child back to the starting point to practice walking slowly in the lot and looking both ways for cars as you cross the lot to your car. That's positive practice.

Response blocking: This is a strategy designed to physically prevent someone from engaging in an undesirable behavior. Let's say your child loves spinning in your office chair and continues to do so even after you have asked them to stop. In a response-blocking procedure, you would walk over to them as soon as they started to spin and hold the chair in place. You would literally block them from completing the spinning behavior, resulting in a reduction of the spinning behavior over time.

Corporal punishment: We all carry some idea of this in our heads, whether it's a spanking or a slap on the hand. It is the delivery of physical pain in response to an undesirable behavior. It isn't recommended and is not particularly effective.

TYPES OF NEGATIVE PUNISHMENT

As described earlier, negative punishment is the *removal* of something after a behavior occurs that will reduce the likelihood of that behavior happening in the future. There are only two main types of negative punishment, both of which are common strategies used by teachers, trainers, parents, and caregivers alike.

Response cost: This is when engaging in a behavior causes the loss of a certain amount of a reinforcer. This technique is often used in classrooms to help teachers manage the behavior of all of their students. A parent may use a reward system at home to track their child's behavior throughout the day. They may start with five star magnets on the refrigerator each day, but if the child engages in a problem behavior, one magnet is taken away. The removal of each star is accompanied by a loss of a privilege or specific type of reinforcer. The loss of reinforcers like less computer time or denied access to certain board games or toys is the response cost.

Time-out: Time-out is a temporary form of physical isolation that causes the child to lose access to natural reinforcers like talking to friends or eating dinner with family.

PUNISHMENT VERSUS REINFORCEMENT

Both reinforcement and punishment are strategies used to change people's behavior, whether it's by focusing on increasing positive or prosocial behavior (reinforcement) or decreasing disruptive or undesirable behavior (punishment). So which strategy is better?

Punishment is a common tactic: Research suggests that more than 94 percent of parents use some form of punishment as part of their parenting repertoire. However, despite its widespread use, many studies have concluded that punishment not only is less effective than reinforcement, but also has negative long-term effects, such as higher rates of aggression among individuals who receive punishment. This is because the negative tactic used on them becomes a model for their own inappropriate behavior.

A 1994 study from Vanderbilt University assessed 273 kids, some of whom received punishment at home and some of whom did not (Strassberg et al. 1994). The children who received punishment showed greater signs of aggression toward their peers in the form of physical and verbal outbursts, while those who did not receive punishment did not show such aggression. The researchers also talked to parents to assess their goals for punishment and determine if the use of punishment improved the prosocial goals they had for their kids. Interestingly, the researchers concluded that despite the parents' professed prosocial goals for punishment, no prosocial development emerged—in fact, prosocial behaviors *decreased*. Parents often say that they are using punishment as a way to "teach" their child "a lesson," but the main thing punishment teaches kids is that punishment is an appropriate means of communication.

Punishment can also become destructive to the parent-child relationship. This is because a parent who uses punishment—whether it's yelling, spanking, or taking away a cherished toy—is unintentionally teaching their child to associate them with the punisher (in this case, the yelling, spanking, or loss of the toy). Repeated use of punishment can cause your child, through that paired association, to experience *you* as an aversive stimulus and to potentially begin avoiding or fearing you even when you're not punishing them. Punishment also teaches kids that others can be forced to adhere to someone else's will if that person exerts their force upon them—a belief they will then be more likely to enact throughout their development.

As a strategy, punishment at times is quicker to implement than a well-thought-out reinforcement intervention, but the learning that takes place with punishment doesn't last as long as behaviors learned through reinforcement. That's partly because, although punishment is designed to decrease unwanted behavior, it doesn't teach anything about what *should* be done instead. Punishment does not replace that unwanted behavior with a desirable one—it just says no.

It's important to remember that the unwanted behavior that you're punishing still serves a purpose for your child—if they weren't getting something out of the unwanted behavior, they wouldn't keep doing it. Simply punishing the behavior does not make the behavior's purpose go away. For example, say you always spend Sunday afternoons working around the house, in the garage, or catching up on e-mails. Then, imagine your child learns (as kids often do) that one surefire way to get your attention while you are engaged in your Sunday afternoon activity is to act out—by picking a fight with a sibling, for example, or being loudly disruptive. If you punish the acting out without teaching your child a more appropriate behavior to replace it, your child no longer has a way of getting that need for attention met. But the need doesn't go away. This can lead to either a return of the original problem behavior or the emergence of a new disruptive way to get your attention.

Punishment on its own isn't a good way to teach kids (or adults!) how to behave in better, more adaptive ways. Reinforcement, overall, is a much better teaching strategy than punishment, because reinforcement focuses on teaching and reinforcing new skills, while punishment is merely focused on reducing unwanted behaviors. Reinforcement allows parents and other caregivers to start from a strengths-based place of affirmation, shaping and encouraging the kind of behavior that teaches kids the skills they need to get along better in the world.

Use Punishment Sparingly and Mindfully

There may be times when you decide it's necessary to punish certain behaviors. Before you undertake the punishment, however, first ask yourself if the goal could be met using reinforcement instead. If you still feel a punishment procedure is necessary, take steps to ensure that you use it as mindfully and as sparingly as possible. Although there are rare cases in which I would choose to implement a punishment procedure first—for example, if a behavior is dangerous to the child or to other people—punishment should generally be used as a last resort.

Mindful use of punishment also means that it should not be used in isolation, but always in conjunction with a reinforcement plan that will shape the more adaptive behaviors you want to see. All behavior is communication, even the problematic behaviors you are working to reduce. If one behavior is being punished, another alternative behavior should be taught that will allow your child to communicate the same message in an appropriate way. Punishment in isolation doesn't address the reason behind the problem behavior. This requires you to figure out the function behind the unwanted behavior, so you can teach an appropriate skill to take its place.

Always be sure that the amount of punishment you administer is appropriate to the seriousness of the behavior you're punishing—in other words, don't punish too severely, because that can lead to its own behavior problems. The amount of the punishment delivered should be enough to be effective, but "less is more" is a good general rule for punishment. Another thing to watch for when using punishment is the possible occurrence of something called *behavioral contrast*.

Behavioral contrast is when, in a specific environment, a behavior changes in the *opposite* direction than it does in the environment where punishment is being implemented. For instance, if you are punishing your child for interrupting conversations at home, but that same protocol is not being used in other settings, you are likely to see an increase in the interrupting behavior in other settings. To help reduce this, ensure the same punishment procedure is implemented across settings and people.

Before using a punishment procedure, it's also important to understand the reason behind your decision to use it. You never want to use punishment because it's easier for *you*, without closely examining how it's working for your child. One tricky thing about punishment is that it can seem to net you good short-term results in the form of immediate cessation of the problem behavior. For example, if your child screams loudly whenever you talk on the phone, anything that ends that behavior quickly could seem like a good idea.

Punishment often results in a quick reaction from the person being punished and likely causes them to cease the behavior in that moment. The quick cessation of the problem behavior can become a negative reinforcer for the person administering the punishment; the relief you feel when the behavior stops is rewarding and can encourage you to use punishment more in the future. Your ability to quickly stop an unwanted behavior by using punishment negatively reinforces your own behavior, because you "escape" from having to deal with the problem behavior. This feels good to you in the short term, but that doesn't mean it is a good intervention. By being mindful of your own behavior and motives, there is less probability you'll misuse punishment as a means to escape your child's unpleasant behavior.

Finally, you should always have a strategy in place to fade out the punishment over time. Punishment should never be your long-term plan. Remember, punishment alone does not teach new behaviors. That's why it should never be used in isolation and should always be accompanied by the teaching and reinforcing of appropriate replacement behavior.

Mindful Use of Punishment: Mason's Story

Mason was about five years old when I started working with him. He came to my clinic because he was known to engage in a wide array of problem behaviors: verbal protesting, whining, having tantrums, noncompliance, and even temporarily running away from home or school. I treated him with ABA services for about three years.

We worked diligently with Mason and his family to decrease his problem behaviors and were extremely successful until it was time for him to go to summer camp. During the summer months, our clinic held a summer camp with normal school hours during the week so students could continue their learning year-round.

Mason, who was used to getting only 25 hours of therapy per week, was now receiving 40 hours of therapy per week—a much more demanding schedule. He'd always shown some signs of aggression in the form of hitting, kicking, and pushing. However, the frequency of his aggression increased significantly when summer camp started. In an effort to reduce his overall instances of aggression, we started by trying to deliver reinforcement for every behavior he engaged in throughout the day. This could be anything from washing his hands when he was done in the bathroom to even responding with a "hi" to others when they greeted him. In other words, we wanted to catch him being good to create more opportunities for access to reinforcement that was greater than the reinforcement he was receiving from physical aggression.

After five consecutive days of this, we weren't seeing the desired reduction in aggression and decided to implement a short-term punishment procedure using response cost (see page 34). One of Mason's favorite field trips was coming up, and we decided to make him earn it with good behavior. We did this by creating a behavior chart for him with five stars on it. For every instance of physical aggression, one star would be removed from the chart. If Mason still had at least one star by the end of the day, he would be allowed to attend the field trip.

There were some days when he would end up with all five stars, and other days when he would barely have one. However, because the field trip was such a huge reinforcer to him, the negative punishment procedure worked to help reduce his instances of physical aggression. Over time, we were able to fade out the response cost, because Mason learned overall that engaging in problem behavior was synonymous with the removal of preferred activities. He was even able to attend the field trip with his peers and had a great time. We have not had to use the positive punishment procedure with him since then, as it was successful in reducing his problematic behavior.

YOUR ACTION PLAN

Now that you have a better understanding of how best to use punishment, when, and for how long, here's an opportunity to apply what you have learned and use *negative* punishment to change your child's behavior. (Refer back to page 32 if you want a refresher on positive and negative punishment before you begin.) For this activity, you will be using response cost as the punishment procedure.

First, pick a behavior you want to decrease. Your behavior goal should be objective, simple, and measurable—i.e., you should be able to easily define what success will look like. When you talk to your child about the plan, use positive and goal-oriented language, rather than emphasizing the "punishment" part. For example, prompt your child with, "Instead of whining when you're tired, calmly ask to take a break." This is much more positive and instructive than telling them, "If you whine, you won't get to go to the movies tonight." Your child will be made aware of the consequence later on, but you do not want the rules you set up to sound negative; you want them to sound positive and achievable.

Determine the time interval during which you will implement the punishment procedure. Base the duration of time during which your child is expected to engage in appropriate behavior on their developmental ability. For instance, with a younger child, the time interval may be four to five minutes, whereas with teenagers or adults, it may be an entire week.

To set up your action plan, you will need one glass jar or clear container and 10 marbles. You will begin your action plan by placing all 10 marbles in the jar. The goal will be for your child to have at least one marble remaining in the jar at the end of your selected time interval so they can access their chosen reinforcer. Each time your child engages in the target behavior you are attempting to decrease, remove one marble from the jar. The removal of the marble is an example of a negative punishment procedure.

It is important to note that each interval should be created independently from the others. That means that no matter what happens during the previous interval, the start of a new interval is the start of a new opportunity.

Note: Marbles cannot go in to the "negative," meaning once they are all gone, a new interval begins. Marbles also do not roll over to the next interval. This means that if your child has three marbles left at the end of an interval, these three marbles cannot be added to the 10 marbles present in the next interval.

TAKING YOUR MEASUREMENTS

Let's go through the steps you'll need to take to start implementing your plan of action. In the sample data sheet to follow, you will see how this all plays out.

1. Make sure your child knows what behavior you are working to *decrease* and is aware of the consequence that will follow if they engage in the problem behavior.

2. Create a data sheet with three columns. Label the first column "Intervals," and number the rows 1 through 10. Label the second column "Number of Marbles Left" to record the remaining number of marbles at the end of each interval. In the third column, record whether that interval was correct (+) or incorrect (–) so you can easily calculate your data at the end of each day.

3. Have a stopwatch or timer on hand so you can accurately determine the beginning and end of each time interval. Set the timer equivalent to the interval of time you are monitoring behavior for.

4. For each interval of time that the problem behavior does not occur, deliver a reinforcer. For each time the problem behavior does occur, remove a marble.

5. If there are marbles remaining at the end of your interval, score that interval as correct (+), regardless of how many marbles are present, and deliver the reinforcer. If, at the end of an interval, there are no marbles remaining, then that interval is incorrect (–) and your child does not receive the reinforcer.

6. You will want to have at least 10 different intervals to collect enough data and determine if your procedure is effective (meaning that the problem behavior decreased over time). To score your data, divide the number of correct intervals by the total number of intervals (e.g., 6 correct intervals divided by 10 total intervals equals 60 percent). If your score is 80 percent or higher, you can deduce that the punishment procedure is likely effective.

In the sample sheet on page 42, three intervals have been completed, which still provides some useful information.

Sample Response Cost Data Sheet

INTERVAL #	NUMBER OF MARBLES LEFT	RESULTS (+ OR -)
1	0	-
2	2	+
3	5	+

Based on this data sheet, you can see that of the three intervals, the child lost all of their marbles during the first one but showed improvement in subsequent ones. We can tell that the child improved not only by the correct signs, but also by the remaining number of marbles. The greater the number of marbles left, the fewer times the child engaged in the problem behavior during the interval. Although you would continue running the program beyond three intervals, this particular data would be calculated by dividing two by three, since we have two corrects out of three total intervals, to arrive at the percentage.

TAKEAWAYS

- Both positive and negative punishment are behavior reduction strategies with various implications for their use.
- If used, punishment must be carefully integrated into a behavior change plan and can be used to reduce the presence of certain unwanted behaviors.
- Punishment is only effective in short-term scenarios, due to unwanted effects on the parent-child relationship and increases in child aggression.
- Punishment should be used mindfully and sparingly to avoid the possible unwanted side effects it can cause.
- Punishment should never be used in isolation but, rather, accompanied by a skill-building program that will teach appropriate, adaptive behaviors to take the place of the problem behavior.

CHAPTER FIVE

Extinction: A Powerful Alternative to Punishment

WHAT IS EXTINCTION?

Extinction is another powerful procedure to change behavior. It's a strategy in which we stop reinforcing a behavior that used to be reinforced, with the goal of decreasing that behavior over time. Extinction is an extremely effective way to reduce unwanted behaviors without having to use punishment. Rather than focusing on punishing an unwanted behavior, extinction involves identifying which reinforcers are encouraging the unwanted behavior and then decreasing the problem behavior by eliminating its sources of reinforcement.

Let's look at a very simple example of how extinction might work in your daily life. Upon entering a dark room, you would most likely turn on a light switch. The behavior of turning on the light is maintained by its immediate reinforcement—the light comes on, and you can see better. Now, imagine that one day you try the switch and the light doesn't come on. You may try to get it to work by flipping it on and off repeatedly, but to no avail. What will probably happen next is that when you enter that room, you'll stop flipping on the light switch, at least until you try changing the lightbulb. See how powerful extinction can be? It took just one instance of removal of the usual reinforcement for you to completely change your behavior.

When parents and other caregivers are first introduced to extinction, they're often told to "just ignore the behavior and it will go away." Although some forms of extinction include ignoring the behavior, it doesn't always begin and end there. The way you implement extinction will depend on the function, or purpose, of the behavior you are extinguishing. If the problematic behavior is being reinforced by your or another caregiver's attention, it would make sense to start by simply withholding that attention to see if that's sufficient to reduce or eliminate the behavior you're targeting.

In many cases, simply ignoring the behavior may do the trick. An example of this would be if your child continues to interrupt your conversations instead of asking for attention appropriately. Extinction in this instance would mean ignoring the interrupting behavior so you don't continue to reinforce it by paying attention every time your child interrupts you. In cases where a problem behavior, such as yelling or otherwise having a tantrum, is being used to avoid or escape a situation your child doesn't enjoy, using extinction means preventing that avoidance behavior from occurring. Let's say you ask your child to eat all of their vegetables, and they have a tantrum because they don't want to. Implementing extinction means still following through and making sure they eat their vegetables before they do anything else once the tantrum is over, however long the tantrum may be. Remember, what you're teaching your child in this instance is that having a tantrum won't get them out of the task they're trying to avoid.

Like punishment, extinction is best used in conjunction with some kind of reinforcement system so you're teaching them what *not* to do, while providing lots of reinforcement for the things they should be doing instead.

WHAT CAN I USE IT FOR?

At this point, you may be thinking that extinction sounds pretty similar to punishment—both are designed to decrease the targeted behaviors, so the outcome is the same, right? While they do both result in a decrease in the targeted behavior, extinction and punishment get there in very different ways.

Punishment assumes we're making some kind of change in the child's environment to get a reduction in the unwanted behavior. We're either adding something or taking something away to make the behavior decrease. So, if your child is acting out, you could either give them extra chores (positive punishment) or take away their device (negative punishment) in the hope of reducing future tantrums. Extinction, on the other hand, is more of a nonevent—nothing that is either reinforcing *or* punishing follows the problem behavior. It sounds almost too simple to be true, but extinction is highly effective, and the results can be amazing.

Let's take a look at an example of this principle at work to better illustrate the difference. Say you have a friend over and your child continuously interrupts your conversation by blurting things out without saying, "Excuse me," or tapping you on the shoulder to get your attention. A positive punishment procedure in this case could be verbally reprimanding your child, while a negative punishment might be taking away a special privilege. An extinction procedure, however, would be ignoring your child's interruptions so the attention-seeking behavior is not reinforced, which will cause that behavior to decrease over time.

Another scenario that could benefit from extinction would be if your child is engaging in problem behavior because they want to stop by their favorite fast food restaurant on the way home. When you drive past the restaurant and continue to your street, your child may become physically or verbally aggressive. Placing this behavior on extinction means continuing to deny access to the item, despite their engaging in the behavior. During moments like this, parents often give their child what they are asking for to try to end the acting out as quickly as possible. However, every time you do that, the behavior you're trying to get rid of is getting reinforced; so it will likely increase in frequency in the future. By understanding the reason, or function, behind the behavior, you can determine how to use extinction in a helpful way.

Although both extinction and punishment will result in similar outcomes if implemented correctly, among ABA professionals and others who work with kids with autism, extinction is the preferred method of intervention. An intense or excessive punishment procedure applied for a prolonged period of time can be unethical, while extinction is a nonevent and is therefore never intense or harsh in nature. And, as I mentioned previously, punishment can lead to a rupture in the parent-child relationship, because it can cause you, as the administer of punishment, to become aversive to your child. This can lead to physical or emotional avoidance of you as a parent, which can be hard to remedy. Extinction may mean that you are withholding reinforcement, but the procedure is temporary and doesn't result in your becoming associated with aversive experiences.

Riding Out the Storm, a.k.a. the "Extinction Burst"

If you've ever heard the saying, "This will get worse before it gets better," you already know a thing or two about what we call the *extinction burst*. An extinction burst is what happens when you first introduce an extinction procedure—that is, when you suddenly stop reinforcing something that, up to that point, had been getting your child what they wanted.

The introduction of extinction usually results in a sharp (but short-term) increase in the problem behavior, as if your child can't believe it isn't working anymore. Remember the example of the light switch that doesn't work? The first instinct in that situation is to repeatedly flick the switch on and off to confirm that the reinforcer—the light turning on—is no longer available. That's the extinction burst in a nutshell. When it's a matter of a light switch, the burst is no big deal. But when the extinction burst takes the form of your child doubling down on a disruptive behavior like yelling or throwing toys, it can be pretty stressful for you. Just remember that it's called a "burst" for a reason. The burst of responding, while sometimes intense, is pretty short-lived.

You'll know an extinction burst is happening when the behavior you've stopped reinforcing temporarily increases in frequency, intensity, or duration. The length of the extinction burst will vary based on your child, the type of behavior, and how long your child has been getting reinforced for engaging in the undesirable behavior.

Parents often worry when they see this sharp increase in the behavior, because they think it's a sign that extinction isn't working. But, in fact, the opposite is true. Extinction bursts are actually a sign that improvement is on the horizon; they let you know that your child has noticed the new intervention and it's already changing their behavior. For instance, let's say your child has a tantrum every time they want extra computer time. Until now, you've been giving in after 10 or 15 minutes and allowing them extra computer time to get them to calm down and stop disrupting your home life. In other words, you've been unintentionally reinforcing the tantrums, which may have grown more frequent as a result.

The day you introduce an extinction procedure is the day you decide you won't give in, no matter how long the tantrum lasts. On that first day, you can expect it may last a while—10, 15, or even 30 minutes. Think about the situation from your child's perspective: Up to now, their only experience is that you give in after a certain amount of time has passed, so they have every reason to believe the tantrum will work if they just keep at it. They may have a longer tantrum, the tantrum may be more intense, or the tantrums may happen more frequently. Think of this as a test to see if perhaps more intense behaviors will get them what they want.

The important thing to do here is to remain consistent and stick to your extinction procedure. You just have to ride out the burst, knowing it will pass. If the problem behavior becomes more intense or longer in duration and, in response, you end the extinction procedure and give in, you've now taught your kid that they can get what they want by engaging in the problematic behavior *even more*. That's definitely not a lesson you want them to learn. However, if you commit to the extinction procedure, you will definitely see a decrease in the behaviors you're working to reduce, and the change may start happening sooner than you expect.

Extinction is a highly effective strategy, but consistency is key. It is also important that everyone working with your child—teachers, trainers, and other family members—is aware of and on board with the procedure as well. If you're using extinction but your spouse or other caregivers are not committed to the plan, this will also teach your child behaviors you don't want them to learn; e.g., never tantrum with Dad, but *always* tantrum with Mom.

At times, implementing an extinction procedure can seem overwhelming; you might feel guilty for saying no, or you might worry that you're causing your child's emotional outburst. In these moments, it's important to have a partner or buddy to rely on when you feel overwhelmed or need a break or a place to vent your frustrations. Whatever the case may be, having support can alleviate some of the stressors that may arise as you commit to helping your child realize long-lasting behavior change.

It's also important to note that once the extinction procedure is set and the problem behavior has decreased, you may at some point experience *spontaneous recovery*. Spontaneous recovery is when a previously extinguished behavior temporarily reappears after some time. This is normal

Extinction in Action: Dalia's Story

Six-year-old Dalia's parents came to my clinic because, whenever Dalia got angry, she would curse loudly to anyone in her vicinity. Naturally, her parents found this embarrassing and were desperate to get her behavior under control. After collecting some baseline data and getting background information from her parents, we were able to deduce that Dalia's cursing was a guaranteed way to get her lots of attention from her parents, peers, and anyone who happened to be nearby. She seemed to love the extreme reactions she got from people who were shocked to hear such salty language coming from a little girl.

Extinction, in the form of ignoring her cursing, seemed like the best intervention to start with. Dalia's parents were apprehensive at first, because they felt like ignoring the cursing was just letting her get away with bad behavior. But they agreed to try extinction, starting in their home, since it was a more controlled environment, where they wouldn't have to worry about the reactions of strangers. To start, we created a plan in which we ignored any instances of cursing by not engaging in eye contact, physical touch, or conversation with Dalia until she stopped and asked to speak to us appropriately.

At first, this caused Dalia to swear more, and louder, shouting curse words at the top of her lungs. This extinction burst lasted about a day and a half, and her parents and I remained consistent as her behavior escalated. With enough support from me, Dalia's parents remained committed to our plan and never even looked at Dalia, no matter how extreme her cursing got. Once Dalia realized that her loud cursing was ineffective, she began changing the curse words she used to ones with more shock value. This took her parents by surprise, because they'd never heard their daughter use such vulgar words, and they worried that the extinction wasn't working. But, together, we rode out Dalia's extinction burst.

After two days of very loud and vulgar cursing, Dalia's behavior began to change. Her overall instances of cursing decreased dramatically, and she started to show more socially appropriate behaviors, like tapping her parents on the shoulder to let them know when she was upset and even asking for breaks when she felt frustrated by something. I explained to her parents that although her cursing seemed to be cured, there was still the chance of spontaneous recovery, so they should be ready to revert back to the original extinction plan. Lo and behold, about two months after we had reached Dalia's behavioral goal, her parents told me she'd gotten frustrated and started cursing while working on a puzzle. They were thrilled to report that they weren't caught off guard and put the behavior on extinction right away.

It's been about two years since I worked with this family, and Dalia's parents tell me that she hasn't cursed again since progressing past her spontaneous recovery.

and does not mean your extinction plan isn't working. When this happens, however, it is important to make sure you still follow through with your extinction procedure as usual.

If the behavior increases during the spontaneous recovery and you don't continue to respond with extinction, there's a chance the behavior will return to its previous rate, strengthened by your reinforcement. Similar to the extinction burst, think of spontaneous recovery as a test to make sure you're still committed to your extinction plan. If you stick to the program, the spontaneously recovered behaviors will fade quickly.

YOUR ACTION PLAN

Now that you know a little more about extinction, it's time to put this strategy to use with your child. As you did in the previous chapter, identify a problem behavior you would like to be the target for your extinction procedure. An example goal would be "a reduction of verbal protesting to zero to one instance per day."

Once you've chosen a behavior you want to reduce and have made sure it is both observable and measurable, determine the function of the behavior you are working on reducing. If the behavior you're targeting is one that helps your child get something they want or engage in a preferred activity, the function is *access*. If the behavior is something that allows them to avoid unwanted situations, the function is *escape*. If the behavior is something that gets them attention, the function is *attention*.

Create your plan for extinction based on the function of the behavior. These are the extinction protocols for each function:

Access—Your child does not get access to the thing they want until they engage in more appropriate behavior and can ask nicely.

Escape—You will not allow them to escape from whatever the situation is, regardless of how long the behavior lasts. For example, if they have a two-hour tantrum because they don't want to do 10 minutes of homework, at the end of the tantrum, you will still require them to complete 10 minutes of homework before they get to do anything else.

Attention—Ignore that behavior until it is over. The only time you will grant attention is when the attention is asked for or sought out in an appropriate way.

Keep in mind that the problem behaviors you are working on now have served a purpose for your child in the past and have been rewarded regularly. They are used to getting what they want, and all of a sudden, that is no longer happening. This can cause them to engage in other problem behaviors that will serve the same function. These should be placed on extinction as well.

As you begin implementing your new procedure, be physically and mentally prepared for an extinction burst. Clear the surrounding area of things that can be used as part of the problem behavior, let people around you know what you are doing so they don't inadvertently reinforce the behaviors you are trying to extinguish, and stay strong. Remember, it will get worse before it gets better. But that just means your plan is working, and the extinction burst will be over before you know it.

TAKING YOUR MEASUREMENTS

With your behavior goal established and your plan of action in place, you are ready to start collecting data. This data sheet will be slightly different from the others you've done so far, because you are measuring frequency and duration differently.

1. Set up your data collection procedure and data sheet based on whether you are working on duration or frequency, as shown in the sample data sheets.

2. Before you start the extinction procedure, take baseline data. By taking baseline data, you are better able to see how much progress is being made overall. Collect at least three days of baseline data on the problem behavior. For example, if you are seeking to extinguish verbal protesting, your first three days will include a simple tally of how many times your child verbally protests without an extinction procedure being implemented.

3. Once you have your baseline data, start implementing your extinction procedure and monitoring changes in behavior. Record the frequency or duration, as appropriate, on your data sheet.

4. If your goal is a certain number of instances per day, the behavior goal is considered mastered if it occurs at or below the target number of instances per day for five consecutive days. If your behavioral goal is duration, then the behavioral goal can be considered mastered if your child engages in the behavior for any duration lower than your goal.

When you've taken these steps, your data sheet may look like one of these two examples:

Sample Frequency Extinction Data Sheet

For: Verbal protesting
Behavior Goal: Verbal protesting will only occur zero to one time per day for five consecutive days.

DAYS	FREQUENCY
Baseline 1	2
Baseline 2	3
Baseline 3	2
Extinction Day 1	4
Extinction Day 2	5
Extinction Day 3	1
Extinction Day 4	1
Extinction Day 5	0
Extinction Day 6	1

Sample Duration Extinction Data Sheet

For: Crying
Behavior Goal: Crying will not occur for more than four minutes for five consecutive days.

DAYS	DURATION (MINUTES)
Baseline 1	7
Baseline 2	6
Baseline 3	8
Extinction Day 1	10
Extinction Day 2	7
Extinction Day 3	6
Extinction Day 4	4
Extinction Day 5	5
Extinction Day 6	4

The goal for the frequency data sheet was a reduction of behavior to zero to one instance for five consecutive days. The baseline shows the behavior was happening two and three times per day, leaving room for improvement. It is important to note that on the first two days of the extinction procedure, behavior went up and was then followed by a decrease. That temporary increase was the extinction burst. Similarly, the first three days on the duration data sheet also illustrate the presence of an extinction burst.

In both cases, you can see that the behavior decreased shortly after the burst. If you implement the extinction plan and remain consistent, your data will likely display the same trend, but now you know what to expect and will be prepared to handle it.

TAKEAWAYS

- Extinction is a behavior reduction strategy that's different from punishment and reinforcement, because it is a *nonevent*, rather than an environmental event in the form of the addition or removal of something.
- The application of extinction varies based on the function of the behavior you are seeking to extinguish, but it will always result in a decrease of that behavior over time.
- The beginning of any extinction procedure will likely be accompanied by an extinction burst, a temporary increase in the target behavior, which lets you know that your intervention is working.
- As with any behavior change procedure, extinction requires consistency and can pave the way to amazing behavioral change success.

CHAPTER SIX

Differential Reinforcement:

Reduce Problem Behaviors and Reward Good Ones

WHAT IS DIFFERENTIAL REINFORCEMENT?

Differential reinforcement is a combination of both reinforcement and extinction procedures. The goal of differential reinforcement is to simultaneously increase positive behaviors and decrease problem behaviors—all with the same powerful intervention. This is an important component of any good behavior change program, because it's the only procedure that covers both the behaviors you're working to increase and those you're hoping to reduce. It allows you to teach new skills to help your child meet their needs, while reducing socially inappropriate behaviors that could get them into trouble.

Most of us already use differential reinforcement without even realizing it. Let's return to the example of your attention-seeking child who keeps interrupting your conversation inappropriately. If they are interrupting while you or your friend are talking as a way to get attention, this is the behavior you would put on extinction by ignoring it. Now, even though the interrupting and excessive talking is being placed on extinction, you would still want to ensure that your child is allowed to share their thoughts when attention is sought in an appropriate way. So, when they say, "Excuse me," or tap on your shoulder and wait to be acknowledged, you would reinforce that behavior by letting them share their thoughts or praising them for not interrupting. That is a classic example of differential reinforcement—ignoring the problem behavior but providing lots of reinforcement for acting appropriately.

Let's consider one more example. Imagine you've been teaching your child to tie their shoes. They are still having difficulty with certain steps, but they typically won't ask for help. Whenever it's time to tie their shoes, they verbally protest and fall to the ground. The first step is to make sure your child knows what alternative forms of behavior are acceptable and what behaviors will not be reinforced. For instance, if this is the first day of your differential reinforcement procedure, you can say, "I know some of the steps in tying your shoes are hard for you, so if you need help, you can ask me nicely. If you whine or complain, I'm not going to help you."

Now that you have set the precedent, your child knows what will and will not work with you—now it's your job to stick to it. When they start to whine or complain, don't respond by trying to help them or by acknowledging their behavior, because your goal is to decrease these behaviors through extinction. However, if they need help and ask you in an appropriate way, you can let them know that you liked how they asked, and proceed to help them.

If you're consistently reinforcing appropriate requests for help and consistently extinguishing inappropriate requests for help, you will start to see that the undesirable behaviors will decrease as the desirable behaviors start to increase. If you remain focused and consistent, differential reinforcement will work like a charm.

ANOTHER GOOD ALTERNATIVE TO PUNISHMENT

By now, you know that reinforcement and extinction are preferred behavior change strategies over punishment. So naturally, differential reinforcement, a blend of these two procedures, is also another great, highly effective alternative to punishment procedures. As discussed earlier, it's a far more powerful teaching strategy to help your child learn what you want them to do, rather than simply punish them for the things they do wrong.

Differential reinforcement incorporates the training and reinforcement of positive behaviors, while punishment does not. And since differential reinforcement reduces negative behaviors through extinction, you skip all the negative consequences of exposing your child to the aversive experience of being punished. Because there is so much emphasis on reinforcement, it will be much easier to get your child on board and enthusiastic about a differential reinforcement plan. They will have many opportunities to earn rewards.

Another great benefit of differential reinforcement is that you can use it to reduce more than one problem behavior at a time and also increase more than one desirable behavior at a time. So, you'll get more work done in less time, and your child will make faster progress. To illustrate, let's take another look at the interrupting example. Say you have already put "talking out of turn" on extinction and are now reinforcing tapping on the shoulder. Because humans are associative learners, the child will also be learning that similar problem behaviors, like yelling or interrupting other people while they are talking, will likely be placed on extinction, too. That means, by virtue of extinguishing the blurting-out behavior, your child will already be less likely to engage in related behaviors *by association*. These various behaviors may still appear, but they will be a lot less frequent, because it's more reinforcing to engage in behaviors the child already knows will get their needs met. Likewise, they will be more likely to engage in similar desirable behaviors, like saying, "Excuse me," or waiting their turn, because they will understand that these behaviors create more opportunities for reinforcement and result in them getting what they want. In this way, differential reinforcement allows you to build multiple skills at a time, while reducing multiple problem behaviors at a time.

Although this may not pertain to you if you have only one child, differential reinforcement is very efficient to do in group settings, because you can target skill building and behavior reduction in multiple people at once. How this works is, if one person in the group interrupts to gain attention, you would withhold attention from the entire group (when appropriate) until someone in the group engages in acceptable attention-seeking behavior. In this way, the whole group has an opportunity to learn what will and will not work, and they are more likely to engage in the behavior that will get their individual and group needs met. How would this work in your home? Here's an example: If you have three children who are all bickering over a particular toy and are unwilling to share, you can take away the toy until one of the children shares an idea with the group for how they can all play nicely with the toy together. Then, you return the toy to that child and verbally praise them for behaving cooperatively. All the while, the other two kids will be learning the same lessons just by watching things unfold.

DRO: IT'S A TWOFER!

There are several different types of differential reinforcement procedures, but we are going to focus on *differential reinforcement of other behaviors* (DRO). DRO is a type of differential reinforcement where the delivery of a reinforcer depends on the *absence* of the problem behavior. This can seem a little confusing at first, so I'll break it down with a few examples.

Let's say your child has the habit of jumping on the couch every few minutes whenever you're paying attention to your other children. Understandably, you find this very frustrating, so you pick jumping on the couch as your target behavior for reduction. Using a DRO procedure, you could say that for every 90 seconds your child isn't jumping on the couch, you'll give them a reinforcer for any appropriate behavior they're doing during that time—even if it's just sitting quietly or sharing a preferred toy with their sibling.

As long as your child isn't jumping on the furniture, basically any prosocial behavior they engage in qualifies for reinforcement. Since the behavior you're working to reduce is attention-seeking, your child will be happy to receive the reinforcer from you and get their attention needs met in a positive way. Conversely, if your child jumps at any point within the 90-second period, no matter the duration or intensity, the jumping is ignored, and they will not receive a reinforcer at the end of the interval.

With DRO, you're combining the powers of reinforcement and extinction to effectively shape behavior in two directions at once: reducing negative behaviors and strengthening positive ones. As this procedure should be done continuously during the time frame you establish, when you set out to do a DRO training—say, for an hour between homework and dinner—it's important to create an action plan that allows you to keep track of the passage of time; on-time delivery of the earned reinforcers is a crucial part of any DRO procedure.

You also have to take care when using DRO to make sure not to accidentally reinforce other problem behaviors that occur during the timed interval. For instance, if your child isn't whining but *is* throwing toys across the room, delivering a reinforcement because they are not whining could potentially reinforce the throwing behavior. One way to reduce the likelihood of accidentally reinforcing other problem behavior is by shortening the timed interval so your child has less time to potentially engage in other problem behaviors. Another solution would be to incorporate the co-occurring problem behaviors into your DRO plan by also putting them on extinction.

Keep in mind that differential reinforcement will only work if you can deliver reinforcers that are *more powerful* than the reinforcement your child gets from engaging in the problem behavior. Your reinforcers should also be available immediately and should be paired with social praise that describes which desirable behaviors your child engaged in that helped earn that reinforcer. You want the reinforcer to be something that is easy to earn, easy to give, and very exciting to have.

Over time, the problem behaviors your child was once engaging in will decrease, because there will be nothing as rewarding or exciting as the reinforcers or the positive attention they get from engaging in prosocial behavior. In this way, DRO can be a huge game changer in your behavior change strategy.

YOUR ACTION PLAN

Differential reinforcement is a fun procedure to introduce to your behavior change strategy because of how quickly you'll see results. It allows you to use two techniques in tandem: extinction and reinforcement. This activity will likely be easier for you to complete, since you have already implemented each of these procedures individually.

Begin by selecting a behavior to reduce. Once again, it must be a behavior you can clearly define and that is both observable and measurable. Next, make a list of positive behaviors your child frequently engages in that you can reinforce throughout the procedure.

Since you'll be using a DRO procedure, you'll also need to decide on a time interval that must pass before you reinforce positive behavior. A good rule of thumb is to measure how much time typically passes before a problem behavior occurs, and set your time interval to end before that interval elapses. For instance, if your child typically hits his peers every two minutes, you may set your interval for every one and a half minutes. That way, you're increasing your child's chance of success by strategically decreasing the possibility that they will engage in the problem behavior before the interval elapses. The more reinforcement opportunities you create, the faster your child will learn.

In this example, you have now established that your goal is to reduce instances of hitting by reinforcing instances of appropriate behaviors that occur during the interval. Keep in mind that you are not reinforcing *during* the interval, but right after it ends. Moreover, you will only deliver reinforcement if no problem behaviors occur during that interval. If unwanted behaviors do happen during the time interval, you will withhold all reinforcement and start a new interval.

Now that you have an idea of what DRO looks like in practice, I'll walk you through a more detailed example: Let's say your child's target behavior for reduction is interrupting when others are talking. The interrupting tends to happen every 1 minute and 15 seconds, so you decide to set your DRO interval to 1 minute. You set a silent, repeating one-minute timer on your watch so you know when the intervals begin and end, and then you begin your DRO procedure.

Every time your child interrupts when others are talking, you know that you will not deliver a reinforcer at the end of the interval. However, if your child has *not* interrupted after one minute, you will deliver reinforcement for any other positive behavior (for example, placing his napkin on his lap at the dinner table) that occurred during that minute.

To make sure your DRO procedure is working, you'll also need to record the number of times per interval that the interrupting behavior happens. For instance, if your child interrupted seven times during the one-minute interval, your data would have seven tallies or the number seven. If the behavior you're targeting, however, is happening at a very high rate per interval, recording how many times it happens may be difficult. In this case, you do not have to record how many times it occurred; instead, you will note with plus (+) or minus (−) to indicate if the behavior did or did not occur during that interval. Once the behavior reduces to a more manageable level, you may decide to record the number of occurrences during each interval for more detailed data on your child's progress.

Differential Reinforcement in Action: Dwayne's Story

Ten-year-old Dwayne was brand-new to ABA therapy. He was newly diagnosed with autism, and his parents were eager to start services. As I was doing the initial interview and gathering the background information, Dwayne's parents told me that one of his biggest problem behaviors was walking across other people's lawns whenever they went for a family walk around the neighborhood. Although this seemed like a small problem to me, Dwayne's parents told me it was a source of great distress, because their neighbors were complaining.

They felt sure that Dwayne understood when they told him to stop walking on their neighbors' lawns, but his behavior didn't change. In fact, they felt that the more they told him to stop, the more he'd misbehave. I decided to accompany them on a walk, and I observed something interesting: During the family walk, both parents were on their phones making calls, sending text messages, and responding to e-mails. They seemed completely zoned out and disengaged. The only time they paid sustained attention to Dwayne was when he was walking on the neighbors' lawns and they were trying to get him to stop. I also learned that Dwayne's parents had such hectic work schedules that their family walk was one of the only times they spent together during the week. For most of the week, Dwayne was with a babysitter, so the family walk was a rare opportunity for Dwayne to spend time with his parents.

Once I realized that Dwayne's behavior was a bid for his parents' attention, I was able to create a differential reinforcement plan that could help them. Our first rule was that the family walk would be a time during which Dwayne received undivided attention from his parents. The strategy was for Dwayne's parents to give him social praise and a high five to acknowledge how well he walked on the sidewalk without having to be told (the desired behavior) and ignore any instances of him walking on the grass (the problem behavior). For this to work, we also informed the neighbors of the plan so they would not inadvertently reinforce walking on lawns by coming out of their homes or otherwise drawing attention to it.

It took only three days until Dwayne was no longer walking on the grass, because he was receiving as much attention and praise as he wanted by walking on the sidewalk! Family walks became a much more enjoyable activity when they all could spend uninterrupted quality time together. Dwayne's parents were happy, the neighbors were pleased, and Dwayne was finally getting the attention he needed.

TAKING YOUR MEASUREMENTS

Before you start collecting data on this action plan, you will need an inconspicuous timer or stopwatch. With DRO, you do not want your child to know that you are reinforcing during certain increments, so try to find a silent or vibrating alarm that only you are aware of. Some watches allow you to set repeating vibrating timers. There are also devices that can be worn inconspicuously which will vibrate after a set interval of time has passed. Remember, for a DRO procedure to be effective, it must be implemented consistently.

1. Determine your time interval and target behavior.

2. Create a data sheet that consists of three columns: one where you can list the number of intervals, another where you can record how many times the behavior happened (optional), and the final column where you will use correct (+) or incorrect (–) to record whether your child engaged in the problem behavior during the interval.

3. Begin collecting your data. Although it may be difficult to implement this procedure every minute, do the best you can to record as much data as possible as you go. The more data you have, the more you can monitor patterns of behavior, such as a spike during the extinction burst or a significant drop in behavior after a certain number of trials.

4. As with other goals for mastery, you can consider this goal mastered if your child scores 80 percent or higher across five consecutive days by demonstrating a reduction in the problem behavior.

   Your data sheet may look something like the one on page 63.

Sample DRO Data Sheet

Interval Time: 1 minute
Problem Behavior: Interrupting

INTERVAL #	NUMBER OF MARBLES LEFT	RESULTS (+ OR -)
1	5	-
2	4	-
3	0	+

This data sheet states the problem behavior (interrupting) and includes the interval time being focused on (one minute). In this example, the numbered intervals (1–3) show that this goal has been worked on three times. The number of occurrences went down with each interval, which shows progress. In the third interval, the child received correct (+), based on the absence of the problem behavior, whereas the earlier intervals were marked incorrect (–), based on the presence of the behavior. As with any differential reinforcement procedure, over time the number of occurrences decreased as the number of correct answers increased.

TAKEAWAYS

- Differential reinforcement is unique in that it incorporates both reinforcement and extinction to create a powerhouse of a behavior change strategy.
- This procedure gives you the opportunity to focus on continuously building your child's strengths while using the tools you have learned to decrease target problem behavior.
- DRO allows you to use nearly every desired target behavior your child displays to work on reducing the target problem behaviors in your child's repertoire. In this way, you're able to use your child's strengths to support positive behavior change and improve your child's life.

CHAPTER SEVEN

It's Complicated:
Straightforward Ways to Teach Complex Behaviors

WHAT IS A "COMPLEX BEHAVIOR?"

Think back to when you were first learning to drive. Driving probably seems like second nature now, but learning to drive initially required the mastery of multiple steps and a lot of practice along the way. Behaviors like this—those that are made up of a chain of smaller behaviors—are called *complex behaviors*. One effective way to teach complex behaviors to kids with autism is to individually teach each small step that makes up the "chain" of the larger, complex behavior.

The best way to determine whether the behavior you're teaching is complex is to assess whether more than one step is required to achieve the ultimate behavioral goal. For instance, sliding a flip-flop onto your foot is not a complex behavior; it is a one-step process. However, putting on and tying your gym shoes is a complex behavior, because it requires multiple steps to be achieved. Most of the behaviors we engage in daily fall into the complex behavior category, so it's critical to learn how to teach your child these behaviors efficiently and effectively. Your job is to break down the complex behavior into smaller, manageable steps and then find the most effective way to teach each step.

The process of linking smaller behaviors together to create larger, complex behaviors is called *chaining*. By breaking these complex behaviors down into smaller, individualized teaching units, you can help your child develop independent living skills and vocational skills, and even teach them fun recreational skills, like sports.

There are three fundamental ways to teach complex behaviors: forward chaining, backward chaining, and total task presentation. Let's look at each of these strategies in more detail:

Forward chaining methods start at the very beginning of the chain of behaviors, teaching one step at a time and not moving on to the next step until the previous step is mastered. Let's take the shoe-tying example again. Forward chaining means that you would only work on having your child pick up the laces and make the "X" with them, making sure they've learned how to do this before moving on to the next step of tying the two laces together. If your child cannot do the first step by themselves, then you would train only this step and finish the rest of the chain yourself so your child understands the ultimate goal of the skill they're learning.

Backward chaining means that you, as the trainer, do all of the steps in the behavior chain except the final one. In the shoe-tying example, the last step would be tightening the bow. In other words, you would do all of the shoe-tying steps yourself and hand the laces over to your child so that they can complete the last step independently. Once your child masters the last step, you work backward down the chain of behaviors to step one. The second-to-last step would be tying the bow, and the step before that would be making the "bunny ears." In this way, you continue to work backward until they can independently complete all of the steps necessary to tie their shoes. Backward chaining is typically used with more difficult complex behaviors, because it builds motivation by creating a history of reinforcement for task completion. Sometimes it's more exciting for kids to see their laces tied in a tidy bow than to get reinforced for completing the first step in the behavioral chain.

Total task presentation means you attempt to teach every step in the behavior chain, from beginning to end, at every training session. The total task approach gives your child more opportunities to practice each step, because they are presented with all the steps each time the chain is being taught.

In most situations, total task presentation is the preferred approach, because your child may learn some steps faster than others and can continue to perfect them while working to acquire mastery of the remaining steps. Backward and forward chaining are the methods to use when a skill is too challenging for your child to realistically execute all the steps on their own. You can judge when it will be beneficial to break down complex behaviors into smaller components.

Now that you have some background information on complex behaviors and the chaining process, you will learn how to create your own behavior chains for training purposes.

BREAKING IT DOWN

In my experience training parents and professionals to use ABA strategies, I've found that people tend to underestimate how many steps are needed to complete a complex behavior chain. For instance, one parent claimed her child could independently brush his teeth without any assistance or encouragement. To make sure this goal had been mastered, I asked her to join me in observing him brushing his teeth so we could collect data according to each step in the behavior chain. I realized not only that the child still required prompting with teeth brushing, but also that his mother was surprised by how many steps he was missing in the chain to task completion. In her casual observations, his mother had simply not noticed the missing steps.

The best way to avoid missing steps when creating your behavior chain plan is to carry out each step of the behavior chain yourself and write them down as you go. Let's say you want to teach your child how to cross the street at a stop sign. Before you teach this behavior chain, you would go to a stop sign and record each step as you carry it out, rather than after the entire chain is complete. When you're done, your behavior chain might look something like the following list.

1. Stop at the corner.

2. Look to the right for cars.

3. Look to the left for cars.

4. Check both directions again.

5. Begin crossing when it is safe to do so (e.g., cars have stopped or are not present).

6. Continue looking both ways as you cross.

7. Step onto the curb safely.

Now, it's very likely that most, if not all, of these steps seem like second nature to you as part of the same, not-very-complicated event. However, when we're teaching kids seemingly basic skills like safely crossing a street, we constantly have to remind them of things that are second nature to us, like looking both ways before stepping off the curb.

Another reason to break down and outline a behavior chain is to help you create a proper order in which to teach the components of the skill. If your child begins crossing *before* they look in both directions, then they will not successfully execute the target behavior. By breaking down each step, you can ensure that you're teaching the entire skill correctly and in the correct order, and not inadvertently training your child to make small errors along the way. This helps you avoid having to add additional steps or reteach parts of the chain when you discover that steps have been left out or are not being completed correctly.

WHAT IS SHAPING?

Shaping is another great way to teach complex behaviors. *Shaping* is defined as "the differential reinforcement of successive approximations of a target behavior." That probably sounds pretty technical, but we've actually covered most of these concepts already. In chapter 6, you learned that differential reinforcement is a combination of reinforcement and extinction. In this chapter, you'll see how significant the role of differential reinforcement is in the successful acquisition of new and complex behaviors.

Shaping is a teaching strategy you've probably already used without realizing it. It's commonly used to teach a wide array of everyday skills, from learning to ride a bike to perfecting athletic skills to learning how to spell new words. Shaping is best illustrated through examples, so here's an in-depth one:

The first time a baby stands with support, you deliver reinforcement by cheering, smiling, and giving social praise. What you're reinforcing is not just the act of standing, but the first solid approximation of the target behavior of walking—you have to be in a standing position to do it!

Next, the baby will learn to stand alone and unsupported, setting off the next round of reinforcement. Now that he can stand without support, you no longer deliver reinforcement for standing with support. From now on, you only deliver reinforcement when he stands on his own. One day, you see him taking his first steps while holding on to the wall. In amazement, you cheer louder than ever and let him know how proud you are of him for taking his first steps. That's the next successive approximation to walking, much closer to the target behavior than where the baby started. You now only deliver reinforcement for walking with support, extinguishing standing with or without support, because you now know he's able to do more than just stand.

Once the baby begins walking independently, that's the only behavior you will reinforce, because you want to increase the likelihood that he will always try to walk without support. In this way, you have used shaping to teach and reinforce independent walking.

Differential reinforcement played a role in teaching this behavior, because you reinforced only the behaviors you wanted to see more of and extinguished behaviors you no longer wanted the baby to engage in, like standing while holding on to the wall. If the purpose of reinforcement is to increase behavior, you know that reinforcing each step will motivate the child to repeat that step more and more. If the child continues to receive reinforcement for all the previous steps they have already mastered, they might be less likely to continue learning how to walk, as their need for reinforcement is already being met without doing so.

Shaping is sometimes confused with chaining, because they share some superficial characteristics. The best way to pinpoint the difference is to remember that chaining is training new behaviors, while shaping is the process of modifying behaviors your child is already doing. Remember that chaining involves breaking down one large, complex behavior into smaller behaviors that are taught individually. These are usually new behaviors the child hasn't yet mastered, as in the example of tying shoes. In contrast, shaping is accomplished by molding and keeping them moving toward the goal by only reinforcing behaviors that take them closer to the target. Each successive approximation, or new behavior, that emerges during the shaping process should be one step closer to the target goal.

Shaping allows you to gradually teach new behaviors in a way that is reinforcing and motivating for your child. It's a win-win situation!

WHAT IS PROMPTING?

Prompting is another very useful tool for teaching complex behaviors. Most of us use or are the recipients of some kind of behavioral prompts on a daily basis. A *prompt* is any stimulus, hint, or help that supports the completion of the behavior you're trying to train. For instance, when you're learning to ride a bike, training wheels are a form of prompt because they support learning successful, two-wheeled bike riding. Similarly, flotation devices for people who cannot yet swim independently help them successfully engage in water activities. Put simply, you can think of a prompt as a "temporary helper."

Implementing Prompts

There are multiple ways to deliver prompts. Let's focus on the two most common: *most-to-least* prompting and *least-to-most* prompting. *Most-to-least prompting* is used when we're teaching a new behavior for the first time. Going from most to least just means that you use the most intrusive and hands-on prompt in the beginning, and gradually decrease your use of the prompt until your child no longer needs the additional support.

Using training wheels to learn how to ride a bike is an example of most-to-least prompting. If it's your first time riding a bike and you don't have training wheels, there's a strong likelihood that you'll repeatedly fall or be unable to even get going, which will prevent you from practicing your new skill. You'll likely remove the training wheels once you begin to get the hang of things—meaning, you no longer need the "temporary helper." The more you continue to practice and your skills improve, the less you'll need the prompt of physical support, until eventually you'll be riding unassisted. This is an example of most-to-least prompting: starting with a very strong prompt that you gradually reduce until no prompt is needed.

Least-to-most prompting is commonly used when working on a skill that is already in your child's repertoire. When using least-to-most prompting, start with the least intrusive prompt and work your way up to more intrusive prompts *only if needed*. This method is most effective in helping promote independent completion of the skill you're training.

A familiar example of least-to-most prompting is that of a new driver taking driver's education class. Student drivers often practice in a car that has a steering wheel and brakes on both the driver and passenger's sides of the car. The instructor will allow the student to drive independently, but if the student doesn't brake quickly enough or has trouble turning, the instructor can intervene and prompt in various ways. They may start with a simple gestural prompt, indicating which way the student should turn the wheel, for example. But if they see the student needs more support, they may upgrade to a vocal prompt and finally a physical prompt by taking over steering themselves.

Prompts are only meant to be temporary; otherwise, your child can become prompt dependent. Prompt dependence happens when your child will not start or complete an activity without a prompt, even if they know how to do it. This happens when prompts are used so often that the child gets used to them and often will not engage in the target behavior without them. For instance, if your child knows how to dress themselves but you continue to dress them every morning because you're in a hurry to get them to school, you may find that when you ask them to dress themselves, they wait for you to help or tell them what the next step is, because your prompts have become a salient part of the task. You can reduce the likelihood of prompt dependence by only prompting when your child needs it and by using the least intrusive prompt necessary when you do.

Fading Prompts

Obviously, adults aren't still riding around with training wheels or driving with hyperalert instructors who periodically take over steering. At some point, these prompts were removed, but how was that accomplished? Prompt removal is best done gradually, through a process called *fading*.

Fading is a gradual removal of applied prompts, resulting in the independent completion of the behavioral goal. You cannot say your child has achieved a target behavior until they can engage in the behavior correctly once fading is complete. For example, if you've only ridden a bike with training wheels, you still can't ride a bike independently. To master bike riding as a behavior, you have to fade out the presence of the training wheels and still demonstrate mastery of the skill.

In my work with kids with autism, I often use fading when teaching them to read. Let's say we're working on reading the names of the colors of the rainbow. I'd begin by writing the name of each color boldly in that specific color; so, writing the word *red* with a red pen, *yellow* with a yellow one, and so on. Next, I'd point to each word and ask, "What do you see?" or "What does it say?" The presence of the color acts as a prompt to help remind the child what the word is. Once they can independently state each word when it's written boldly in the target color, the next step is to rewrite each word in the same color but not as boldly, making the prompt subtler.

I would follow this up by rewriting each word in black ink and using the target color to underline each word. We would then practice reading each word until mastery is obtained and they can read all of the words accurately. The last step would entail simply writing the word without any color prompts to make sure that they can still correctly read the word when asked. The fading procedure for this goal would look like this:

1. **Red**
2. Red
3. <u>Red</u>
4. Red

In this example, the red text is gradually faded away until the target behavior can be achieved without the prompt. It's very important that prompts are faded out gradually, as this ensures that your child's level of independence gradually increases with the removal of each prompt level. If you take the training wheels off your bike too quickly, you may not be ready and are more likely to fall and have a bad experience. Likewise, you can end up losing ground if you take away the prompts before your child is ready.

If you fade at a slower, more gradual pace, you allow your child time and space to adjust to the newer circumstances and master each successive skill level. Every ABA intervention strategy should have plans for both prompting and fading procedures to make sure your child is getting the support they need in the short term to achieve the overall goal by themselves in the long term.

YOUR ACTION PLAN

You've learned that complex behaviors are best taught by breaking them down into steps, and you've also learned the various strategies to teach those steps. Now it's time to create your plan to teach a complex target behavior to your child. Your first step is to determine which behavior to teach. The behavior itself will help you determine which strategy is best to use. For example, if the behavior is composed of smaller steps that must be taught in a specific order—as many behaviors are—chaining is likely a good route for you. However, if the behavior you are seeking to teach cannot be broken down clearly into smaller steps (like learning to walk unassisted), you will likely use a shaping procedure.

Let's say you will be teaching your child how to wash their hands, which requires a multitude of steps that must be completed in a specific order. Before you teach the complex behavior, you need to write out each step in the correct order. The first few steps may look like this:

- Approach the sink.
- Turn on the water.
- Adjust the water's temperature.
- Wet your hands under the running water.
- Get one to two pumps of soap, and lather your hands.

Decide which chaining method you will use. With handwashing, total task presentation would be the best option, because it allows your child to practice every single step each time you work together on the complex behavior. Also, due to the frequency with which most children and adults wash their hands, there is a very good chance that some of the handwashing steps are already in your child's skills repertoire.

The final step in your action plan will be to decide whether most-to-least or least-to-most prompting would be more effective. If this is a newer skill for your child, then most-to-least might be best.

Fading in Action: Valentina's Story

I began working with six-year-old Valentina just after she finished first grade. Her parents described Valentina as a bright girl who could read and spell as well as anyone else in her class. However, they were worried she might have to repeat first grade because her teacher didn't want to promote her, due to her extremely poor penmanship skills. Valentina's teacher told me that her writing was so illegible that it was impossible to even read her name written at the top of her homework. In fact, sometimes her teacher couldn't grade her quizzes or assignments, because she couldn't decode their "hidden Valentina messages."

Valentina's parents said they had worked with her daily to improve her hand-writing, but were unsuccessful. I only had about two months to work with Valentina before the decision would be made to hold her back or promote her with her classmates. I decided to start our fading protocol (in this case, most-to-least fading) by writing out each word for her in dark pen so all she needed to do was trace over it—a skill she already had. This allowed me to see that with some practice, she was physically able to hold a pencil steadily and write her sentences legibly.

Valentina loved attention, so I made sure to deliver social praise after each time she traced the letters neatly. Once she'd mastered that phase, I changed the color of my marker from black to gray, then to light green, then to light orange, until all that was left was a very light yellow. As I gradually faded out my prompt, Valentina's writing continued to improve and ultimately became much more legible than when we'd started. Her parents were concerned that once I removed the yellow prompt, her writing would return to being illegible. I assured them that with a little more gradual fading, they'd see that Valentina was more than capable of improving her writing and moving forward with the rest of her class.

In the final phase of fading, rather than tracing out the entire letter, I drew dots to outline each letter and had Valentina connect the dots. Once she mastered this, I removed one dot at a time until Valentina was down to only two dots, then one dot—and then none. At each phase of the fading, she wrote neatly and legibly until she was doing it with no prompting at all.

In the beginning, Valentina needed a lot of support in the form of very strong prompts, but by the end of our time together, she was writing more clearly than she ever had before, much to the surprise of her parents and her teacher. By slowly fading out the visual prompts, Valentina learned how to write neatly and carefully and was well on her way to the second grade.

TAKING YOUR MEASUREMENTS

Now that you've established the behavior to teach and have decided how you will teach it, it is time to start taking your measurements. The following steps are an example of measuring the total task. If you are teaching only certain parts of a task, record only those parts on your data sheet.

1. Write the behavior on the top of the data sheet, and list all the steps involved in performing the behavior, as in the sample to follow.

2. Instruct your child to begin the complex behavior by stating, "Show me how you [name the behavior]."

3. Record either correct (+) or incorrect (–) for each step, depending on whether your child was able to complete that step on their own. For instance, using handwashing as an example, if they approach the sink by themselves and turn on the faucet independently, you would place correct (+) next to both steps. However, if during the third step, you had to point to the soap to remind them to use it, you would put incorrect (–), because that step required a prompt.

4. Continue to work your way through the behavior list, recording either correct or incorrect and prompting as needed. To reduce the possibility of prompt dependency, use least-to-most prompting. For example, if your child has not yet turned on the faucet, avoid immediately turning it on for them (using a physical prompt). Instead, try pointing to the sink to see if that is enough to remind them of the step. Although physical prompts are helpful, they should be used as a last resort.

5. Remember to collect your data as your child completes each step, because it can be difficult to accurately record data if you wait until the entire behavior chain is complete.

6. To calculate your data, count the number of corrects and divide by the total number of steps. For instance, if there are five total steps and four of them were done correctly without a prompt, then your percentage would be 80 percent (4 divided by 5).

7. Decide what percentage correct (+) your child will have to get to prove to you that the skill is mastered and that they can do it independently (remember, this should be 80 percent or higher). Because so many steps must work together to create one complex behavior, it is important that your child has a relative mastery of each individual component.

After you have taken these steps, your data sheet may look something like this:

Sample Complex Behavior Data Sheet

Target Behavior: Handwashing

DATE	STEPS TO BE COMPLETED	COMPLETED INDEPENDENTLY (+ OR -)
8/20	Approach the sink	+
	Turn on the water	+
	Adjust the water's temperature	-
	Wet your hands under the running water	+
	Get 1 to 2 pumps of soap and lather your hands	+

In this example, the first two steps were taken without a prompt, but the child needed to be prompted to adjust the water temperature. The remaining steps were completed independently. In this case, the percentage is 80 percent.

TAKEAWAYS

- Break complex behaviors down into smaller, individualized teaching units, using forward chaining, backward chaining, or total task presentation to teach your child each step of the behavior.
- Differential reinforcement plays a role in shaping, the process of modifying behaviors your child is already doing.
- Prompting is a temporary strategy used to achieve greater behavioral independence; most complex behaviors in our everyday repertoire could not have been possible without the presence and ultimate removal of prompts.
- To reduce the likelihood that your child will become prompt dependent, do not prompt too frequently or too intrusively.

CHAPTER EIGHT

Your Child's Social Skills:

Communicating, Cooperating, and Contributing

THE SPECIAL CHALLENGE OF SOCIAL INTERACTIONS

A hallmark trait of anyone with autism is difficulty forming and navigating social relationships. This is often one of the top concerns parents voice when they receive their children's diagnoses—they worry their children won't be able to make friends or get along in school. Fortunately, there are steps you can take to help identify the underlying struggles that contribute to your child's difficulty navigating social environments.

When I'm working with parents to help their children gain more social skills, I like to focus on specific targets that are interfering with successful social interaction. For example, many kids with autism have a hard time staying on topic in a conversation, while others may have difficulty reciprocating with questions so conversations flow smoothly. By identifying which specific skill your child either is lacking or needs to improve on, you can create a plan to target that directly. Reinforcement is a critical principle to apply here, because your delivery of social reinforcement like smiling and eye contact will also serve as a model for similar types of reinforcement your child will receive from others when they engage in socially appropriate behaviors with peers.

Let's say you are working with your teen on sharing and learning information about another person through conversation. You can use a chaining procedure to break down the different parts involved in having a conversational exchange with peers. Once you've identified the different steps for having a conversation, you can practice them with your teen and deliver reinforcement when they engage in each step correctly, or give prompts when they do not. This is a skill you can continue to practice with them until they have achieved mastery and are able to use the skill with peers and in a natural setting.

For other teens, their lack of spatial awareness (a sense of personal space) may get in the way of their ability to maintain a socially appropriate conversation with peers. By helping your teen practice proper personal space and delivering reinforcement for appropriate responses, you increase the likelihood that they will engage in similar behavior with peers in the future. In this way, you can see how the principles of ABA can still be applied to the development of something as complex as social skills.

In the next two sections, I will discuss induction, generalization, and flexibility to help you better understand the importance of each in the development of appropriate social skills.

The Problems of Induction and Generalization

One of the difficulties that can arise from trying to teach complex social skills to kids with autism is a lack of *induction.* Induction is when we apply one learned response to multiple situations, even if we have never encountered those situations before. People with autism are typically very rule driven and prefer familiar situations. This can make induction difficult, because they may not know how to respond in a novel and unfamiliar situation.

If you are teaching your child to greet others, you would naturally start with teaching them to say hi or hello. In most instances, this would be fine; however, if someone asks your child, "How's it going?" and they simply respond with, "Hi," it is clear that induction has not occurred, as they have only one greeting in their repertoire. When a person's social repertoire is limited, it can negatively affect their ability to engage with others in a socially appropriate way. Induction is an important skill for your child to learn so they are able to respond correctly to a new scenario based on what they have learned from similar scenarios. One way to ensure that induction happens is to teach your child multiple examples of responses. For instance, they could also know to respond with "Hey" or "Great, how are you?" when appropriate.

Another problem that may arise during communication with others is a lack of *stimulus generalization. Stimulus generalization* is the tendency to respond in new settings and around new people the same way we would respond in situations with familiar people and settings. People with autism often demonstrate difficulty generalizing skills across situations and people, even if the response would be exactly the same in the new setting. Let's say your child has mastered conversational skills with everyone at home but not with their peers on the playground. This demonstrates a lack of generalization across settings and people, because even though they have the skills in their repertoire, they are not translating to new scenarios.

Let's say your child learns how to count change at home but cannot do so when they are purchasing an item at the store; the skill of counting change has not been generalized, so you would want to teach counting change in various places. In the same way, teaching social skills requires practice across settings and people, as well as teaching multiple responses for various scenarios. Mastering both induction and generalization will enable your child to engage in more seemingly natural social interactions.

Flexibility Is Key

Flexibility is a very important component in your child's social skills repertoire. Here, *flexibility* refers to your child's ability to "go with the flow," both within conversations and with their routine. It is important to pay attention to your child's ability to engage in flexibility in various areas of their life. If you notice your child has a difficult time being flexible with routines, conversation topics, thoughts or behaviors, or even rules, this is definitely an area to focus on.

A lack of flexibility can take many different forms and will look very different for each person. There are many different areas where children can exhibit rigid behavior at times. But whatever form your child's lack of flexibility takes, it is likely hindering their ability to successfully socialize with their peers. By understanding that each rigid behavior is the result of a lack of *overall* flexibility, you can look at flexibility as the antidote for social success rather than some impossible feat to achieve.

Teaching your child flexibility will be difficult at first, but it can be implemented incrementally. This could mean taking a different route to or from school and helping your child use effective transitioning and coping techniques if this is difficult for them. Practicing flexibility could also include trying a brand-new restaurant, encouraging your child to taste a new food or engage in a new activity, and even changing where your child sits for dinner.

By differentially reinforcing flexible and rigid behaviors in your child, placing some aspects on extinction while reinforcing others, you can simultaneously work to increase their range of flexibility and decrease the frequency of their rigidity. Regardless of your method, your mindfulness and dedication to breaking the rigidity cycle will prove successful.

HE SAID/SHE SAID: TEACHING CONVERSATIONAL SKILLS

Due to the complexity of social interaction, teaching your child conversational skills can be difficult. Complicating matters is the fact that conversational skills and customs vary across cultures, geographical regions, families, ages, and even sometimes across genders. The needs of each individual are as different as the individuals themselves.

For children with autism, there is a range of common areas where they struggle with conversational skills, including perseveration on specific topics, not responding to greetings from others, constantly interrupting others, speaking too loudly or quickly, failing to make eye contact, and even sending too many text messages at once. They may even tend to boss others around. These are just some of the many issues parents are concerned about regarding their children's ability to verbally make contact with peers and potential friends.

Your first step in outlining a plan to improve your child's conversational skills is to decide which behaviors to target, so let's look at some of these common challenges in a little more depth.

Appropriate use of texting is a challenge that is particularly important for teens to work on. I've found that many adolescents with autism have a difficult time engaging in conversation via this medium. They may send too many text messages at once, have difficulty understanding written sarcasm or idioms, or may even overuse typical text slang. One remedy for this is to set a rule where they will only send two messages in a row without receiving a response back. Additionally, if they receive a text with a saying they don't understand, they must check in with a parent or caregiver before responding to make sure the response is appropriate for the conversation.

For other children, not responding to a peer's greeting or not making eye contact with that peer signals to the other person that the child is not interested or does not want to engage in social interaction. A popular intervention used when working with greetings or eye contact is pairing the behavior with a preferred stimulus. Let's say your child loves putty. For the first two days, every greeting they respond to results in the delivery of a small amount of putty by the person who received the greeting. (In this case, the people who are greeting your child are people who know that you are using this intervention.) Because such a highly preferred reinforcer is being used here—the putty, or whatever else your child loves—it is easier to gain compliance and work to improve your child's conversational skills.

If your child is speaking too loudly, too softly, or bossing others around, peers may disengage from the conversation because it can seem like too much work for them. If your child has a greater understanding of empathy and socioemotional reciprocity, you can explain to your child how the policing, volume, and tone of voice can negatively affect the listener, and you can work on that with them.

You are the expert on your child, so you have the opportunity to closely analyze your child's conversational strengths and challenges. Once you have clearly identified each of the conversational skills that are negatively affecting your child's life and require your attention, you can create a plan of action to best support their needs.

GIVE AND TAKE: TEACHING RECIPROCITY

One of the most common diagnostic criteria for autism is a deficit or impairment in socioemotional reciprocity. *Socioemotional reciprocity* is most simply defined as difficulty with "normal" social interactions, like engaging in back-and-forth conversation, and the impairment of the ability to share common interests, express emotion or affect (that is, their ability to express situationally appropriate feelings), or independently initiate interactions with peers.

These deficits can be very challenging to address, because your child may struggle with learning to express reciprocity in ways that appear natural or socially appropriate. For example, your child may have difficulty engaging in reciprocal conversation, as evidenced by only sharing information about themselves and never asking peers questions about themselves. Your child's one-sided conversation habit may not mean they're uninterested in their peers. However, your child's lack of reciprocity likely communicates to their peers that your child isn't interested in building a social relationship with them. Therefore, it is very important to do the best you can to improve your child's socioemotional reciprocity.

To promote this, I've created specific programs for clients to practice reciprocating questions effectively. I start by asking them how they are doing and wait for them to state the correct response. The correct response in this case would be to first respond to my question and then proceed to ask me the same question. Here is an example:

Therapist: "What is your favorite food?"

Client: "Mine is enchiladas. What is your favorite food?"

Therapist: "Thank you for asking!" (Social praise is delivered here as a reinforcer.) "Mine is also enchiladas."

If your child has difficulty reciprocating questions, it may be better to work on a personal information program first. This would entail simply asking them questions about themself (e.g., first and last names, favorite movie, address, phone number, etc.).

A personal information program is important because it not only helps them learn important information about themselves, such as their address and phone number, but also can be used to help them identify their own preferences. These preferences can then be used as conversation starters with peers and opportunities to share information about themselves with peers who have similar interests. Your child's ability to engage in reciprocal dialogue is the gateway through which they're able to make and sustain connections with others.

Teaching reciprocity also means teaching your child to remain quiet when others talk, maintain conversation on a specific topic in appropriate situations, and know how to end a conversation appropriately. Each of these skills is best learned through practice. As the goal of reciprocity is often engagement with same-aged peers, it would be helpful if your child has a similarly aged individual with whom they can practice new skills before generalizing these skills to other peers.

The most important thing to note is that your child must know about themselves and their own interests before they can seek out information from anyone else or find common interests with their peers.

PERSPECTIVE TAKING: TEACHING EMPATHY

Another important skill to teach when working with your child is empathy. Empathy is the ability to understand, respond to, and share in the feelings of another person. It's a common belief that people with autism lack empathy, but that simply isn't true. What people with autism tend to struggle with is *expressing* the empathy they feel. There are many prerequisite skills that must be acquired before a person can demonstrate empathetic behavior, making this nuanced form of expression take longer to learn—often this is true even for people who don't have autism!

Fundamentally, experiencing and expressing empathy requires a person to be capable of taking the perspective of another. Empathetic behavior cannot be demonstrated unless someone is able to recognize the feelings of others by reading their facial expressions, deciphering nonverbal communication, interpreting body language, and understanding complex emotions.

When a person is able to understand these, they are better equipped to also understand the emotional experiences of others, even when they're different from their own.

There are a number of socially recognized ways to demonstrate empathy, which can be trained with some work. For example, I once worked with a child who had difficulty expressing empathy to peers and adults. We first began by having him label the emotions of others based on pictures of their faces. We determined that the only emotion he could independently identify was happiness. Once he mastered this goal behavior, we expanded it by asking him to also state a logical reason why the individual would feel the way they do, as well as share some things he could say or do personally to support them.

We then sought to generalize the behavior by having him respond to the same three questions based on real-life scenarios that would occur among his peers at school, siblings at home, and children at my clinic. With help labeling emotions via facial expression and correctly identifying his own role in the situation, he was able to express empathy to peers and adults. In fact, one week prior to writing this chapter, I accidentally hit my elbow on the wall and said, "Ouch." From across the room, I heard this child yell, "Are you okay?" Now, interpreting the sounds of others without any knowledge of their facial expression was not a skill we taught, but it was a clear indicator that his ability to demonstrate empathy had evolved beyond our initial intervention.

Another benefit of training basic empathy is that it further supports the safety of those around your child. To illustrate, once your child is able to express empathy, they can also respond to others by refraining from engaging in problem behavior when asked to do so. An example of this is a teen who is making a joke about their peer. If the teen understands that their joke is causing the other person discomfort, based on their facial expression or body language, the teen can respond by stopping the joking behavior.

Empathy is a powerful skill in everyone's life. It helps us communicate our needs and desire for connection with others. By teaching empathy to your child who has difficulty expressing it independently, you open up a whole new world of opportunity for human connection.

YOUR ACTION PLAN

The purpose of this action plan, which will be a little different from the others, is for you to analyze your child's individual social needs and use the ABA principles you learned in previous chapters to support social skills development.

The first step in teaching social skills is to identify the mechanisms underlying your child's social challenges. In other words, start by creating a checklist of behaviors that interfere with your child's ability to make and maintain social relationships. If you are having difficulty pinpointing specific skills or behaviors your child needs to work on, you'll find a plethora of information online that categorizes various social skills based on the typical age of skill acquisition.

Let's use the example of perspective taking for adolescents. Although perspective taking is its own complex behavior, there are many complex skills within it that must be mastered for it to be effective—for instance, the recognition of body language and emotions, understanding when others engage in behaviors to be nice or malicious, using appropriate language to express disapproval, accepting and tolerating the similarities and differences of others, and engaging in reciprocal conversation in which empathy for others is expressed. Perspective taking for a younger child might focus on being able to describe the physical features of others, understanding and respecting personal space, using social cues to label emotions, identifying the functions of various community helpers, and also labeling their own preferences. This may look different for your child, depending on their age, developmental ability, and current social skills repertoire.

The most common social skill goals for children and adolescents alike are trading information by using appropriate conversational skills, initiating and exiting peer interactions appropriately, and engaging in prosocial behavior (like cooperation).

When you have made your list of desired goals, organize them in order of simplest to most complex. Once you have identified which preliminary skills must be taught first, your action plan must also include a plan for induction, generalization, reinforcement, and fading. You can increase the likelihood of induction and generalization by teaching your child multiple ways to respond to similar scenarios across settings and people. To increase

The Importance of Social Skills: Jayden's Story

Jayden was a 17-year-old boy who had been diagnosed with autism a year earlier. He told me that he was having difficulty making and keeping friends and wanted to work on his social skills before college. My goal was to determine which parts of his social repertoire were holding him back, focus on complimenting his current strengths, and give him homework to help him feel better prepared for social interactions with peers and romantic interests.

After careful observation of Jayden in multiple settings, I deduced the following: He had a hard time establishing connections with others, because he would talk only about himself. He also had problems understanding personal space, standing either too close to or too far from the person he was speaking to. Jayden also divulged too much personal information too quickly, which often made other people uncomfortable and abruptly ended conversations.

My first goal with Jayden was to work on his ability to engage in reciprocal dialogue. I shared my observations with him and let him know what my goals for our time together were, making sure we were on the same page and were both actively working toward his success. I started by modeling what appropriate reciprocal dialogue was, giving him a script of questions to ask me so I could respond back to him naturally. Jayden could see how much more information he was learning by simply asking a few questions.

To make sure he was listening to my responses, I followed up each role play with a request for a summary of things I had shared about myself. If Jayden answered the questions correctly, I delivered reinforcement in the form of social praise. However, if Jayden got the question wrong, I would use the mild verbal reprimand, "Try again," and provide additional prompting if needed.

Once we mastered Jayden's ability to engage in appropriate two-way conversation, we focused on the amount of information he was divulging about himself. Jayden still experienced some difficulty being able to interpret my nonverbal expressions, so instead of making a face to show disapproval if he shared too much information, I would use a buzzer. After about a week of this, he had mastered his new goal and could both engage in reciprocal conversation and maintain appropriate conversational boundaries.

Our next area to tackle was his sense of personal space, or lack thereof. Jayden was wonderful at math, so I told him to use a two-foot distance as his average space marker when speaking with friends. We initially practiced this a few times with Jayden holding his arms out, and then we began to fade out that prompt across settings—and he was still able to maintain an appropriate distance. Although our time together was cut short because Jayden left for college, his is still one of my favorite success stories, because he gave me an opportunity to apply the principles of ABA to a truly nuanced and complicated set of behaviors that are critical to success in life.

the likelihood of positive social interaction, it will be imperative that various people deliver the reinforcement for each of the responses across settings. This strategy is one that can be done regardless of the target social skill, desired response, or setting.

TAKING YOUR MEASUREMENTS

Because the action plan in this chapter is different from the others, your data collection will be a little more involved than in previous chapters. Setting the criteria for mastery of social skills is more complex, because you may not always have the time to work on specific social goals, which can be time consuming, and you also want to make sure that all goals remain mastered, as many of them will build on each other.

1. Once you have organized the target social skills goals according to priority—for instance, if your child is having difficulty identifying how someone is feeling based on their facial expression, this is a greater priority than being able to respond to another person's emotions—choose which behaviors will be targeted first and create a data sheet such as the one on page 91.

2. Begin your action plan, remembering to include strategies for induction, generalization, reinforcement, and fading. Observe your child as they interact with others with regard to the target goal.

3. Social skills goals may be difficult to score as correct (+) and incorrect (−), because you want to ensure that they are being generalized across settings and with different people. Do your best in various situations and with different people to determine if your child successfully completed what you set out for them to do.

The sample data sheet on page 91 can help you better understand how data is collected across various social skills goals.

Sample Social Skills Data Sheet

SOCIAL SKILLS GOAL	LOCATIONS TARGETED	NUMBER OF INDIVIDUALS	COMPLETED INDEPENDENTLY (+ OR −)
Sharing Information with a Peer	School, home	2	+
Sharing Information with a Peer	Home, park	3	+
Maintaining Conversation	School, home	2	+
Maintaining Conversation	Home, park	3	+
Giving Prosocial Comments	Park, mall	2	+

In this example, the child worked on three different social skills goals, all of which were done without prompting. The first column shows which targets they specifically engaged in. The second column includes each location where the child had an opportunity to engage in the behavior. The third column includes the number of individuals present, which is important for generalization purposes, letting us know that these goals are being targeted in varied settings and demonstrating true mastery. The final column shows that this child was successful in completing the task at hand in each instance.

TAKEAWAYS

- Acquiring social skills can pose a particular challenge for kids with autism.
- Induction refers to a person's ability to respond differently, yet appropriately, in similar situations.
- Generalization refers to a person's ability to respond the same way in different settings and with different people.
- Induction and generalization can be promoted by practicing skills across settings and people, as well as introducing multiple responses to similar scenarios.
- By identifying conversational skills and areas of rigidity that hinder your child's ability to engage socially, you can create a plan of action to achieve the desired outcome.

CHAPTER NINE

It Takes a Village:
Coordinating with Teachers, Trainers, and Other Caregivers

REINFORCING YOUR CHILD'S TRAINING AT HOME

If your child is receiving services at school or another learning center, you were likely asked to continue the work they are doing there at home. Let's talk for a moment about why this is important. Any trainer or health professional your child is receiving services from may only be working with them for brief periods—perhaps even as little as 30 minutes a week, which is less than 1 percent of an entire week. For meaningful learning to take place, it's imperative to do what you can to ensure that your child practices the skills as regularly as possible and that these skills become a regular part of their daily routine. Moreover, you want to be consistent and generalize across settings and people so your child can get the most out of the training.

I have seen children make amazing progress with their behavioral therapists, but their parents do not see those same improvements at home. I once worked with a six-year-old who was verbal but seldom used her words to ask for items or activities. The therapy team at my clinic worked with her regularly to increase how often she would ask for what she wanted. Soon, she was asking for everything in sight, and we made sure to consistently reinforce her new behavior whenever possible.

However, during our group meeting the following week, her parents shared that their daughter was still not vocally requesting items or activities at home. We soon discovered that her parents continued to give her access to her favorite games and activities without requiring her to ask, because it was easier for them. This lack of consistency not only confused their daughter, but also limited our ability to ensure her newly developed skills were practiced in other environments. It also led to an increase in her maladaptive behaviors, because our requests and her parents' requests were different. People will always engage in the behaviors that result in reinforcement, and this child was no different. She did not ask for what she wanted in other settings, because her parents didn't require it at home; and she asked for what she wanted from therapists, because that was the behavior we focused on reinforcing.

Health professionals and other trainers will do what they can to help your child progress, but you are the mechanism of change through which your child has the opportunity to truly harness and practice their new skills.

Working with Specialized Trainers and Caregivers

When you and your child are working with multiple professionals and experts from different fields, you'll often find that each has different goals or intended skill sets they're focused on. Your child's speech therapist may ask you to practice one skill, while their occupational therapist or teacher may highlight something else. At times this can feel overwhelming, especially if you're receiving input from multiple trainers in different areas. Always remember, however, that your support and efforts are exceedingly important to your child's success.

As their primary caregiver, you play a vital role in your child's growth. And now that you've adopted this book's techniques and strategies, you have tools to coach and support your child in ways others cannot. In fact, you might be in a position to show other trainers and caregivers a few strategies for teaching new skills and reinforcing behavior.

At the end of each training session, ask the trainer how your child did, what skills they worked on, and what targets or goals you should focus on during the week to help complement their efforts. You may want to collect data and chart progress as you've been doing to ensure improvements are being made in those areas. Many trainers incorporate caregiver-training goals into their plan, which are goals specially designed to educate parents and caregivers and provide them with tools for in-home training.

If multiple professionals work with your child, encourage them to collaborate and communicate with one another on a regular basis. You may have to facilitate this at first, but the effort will be worth it. For instance, if your child has speech therapy both at school and after school, allow the therapists to communicate with each other to create common goals and work on them consistently. By collaborating, professionals also have the ability to maximize one another's strengths and clinical expertise, which will serve to help your child fulfill their potential.

Even though you're not an expert in certain areas, like vocational training, you have the privilege of serving as the liaison between professionals and can advocate and support your child throughout the process. The bottom line is, if you are not actively reinforcing your child's training in your home or are not on the same page with your child's trainers, the therapies will not work well and, in fact, can even lead to regression of your child's progress. You will always be the most important part of your child's growth process: You are the core of all the supporting services your child receives. When you and all the professionals providing your child with services work together, and you capitalize on all the learning opportunities in the natural environment, the rate at which your child learns and maintains new skills will increase exponentially.

TEACHING TEACHERS: SHARING THE TOOLS OF ABA

Of all the professionals your child has contact with, teachers are often most receptive to learning new information and strategies. All you need to do is take time to highlight how these techniques will improve their ability to manage student behavior and teach effectively.

Teachers are dedicated to creating a positive learning environment and helping their students succeed, but they are limited in their ability to give consistent, undivided attention to each student. The teacher's priority is classroom management; their ability to run their class and teach effectively relies on the degree to which they can maintain an environment conducive to learning for *all* of their students. With this in mind, it is ideal to approach your child's teacher with ideas that aren't complex or time consuming to integrate into their class routine.

Let's say you've decided to start a system at home for your child where they can earn tokens for appropriately gaining attention from others and waiting their turn, rather than interrupting. These tokens can then be traded in for prizes that are based on demonstration of the target behaviors. If getting attention appropriately and waiting their turn are also issues in the classroom, teacher involvement in this strategy would be ideal. The results would also benefit your child's teacher and help them better manage these behaviors in class. You could even give your child's teacher tokens to use so they can also reinforce your child's appropriate behaviors throughout the school day. By choosing a goal your child's teacher is equally invested in and creating a simple system for them to use in the classroom, you provide more opportunities for your child to acquire the desired skills and decrease their maladaptive behaviors in class.

If a teacher is skeptical about getting involved or does not see the benefit of the strategy you're suggesting, it can be helpful to share how much of a decrease in problem behavior or increase in positive behavior you've seen since you started implementing it. Teachers are often not familiar with ABA techniques and strategies, so it's also possible they will feel intimidated or reluctant to try something new, especially if they are comfortable with their way of doing things. This is an opportunity for you to validate their feelings about trying something new, because ABA was once new to you, too. Openly share your success with your child's teacher, but remember that the goal is for the results to speak for themselves.

It is important for parents and teachers to form and maintain a strong, positive partnership for the child's benefit. This facilitates better communication, consistency of intervention, and improvement in targeted behavioral goals. You know a lot about training now and can offer your support and guidance if your child's teacher has any questions. By giving them concise, informative tips and creating a space for supportive dialogue, you increase the likelihood that your child's teacher will be motivated to learn about the skills you're using at home and implement them in the classroom setting.

Advocating for Your Child

In an ideal situation, parents and trainers work together cohesively for the child's benefit. Unfortunately, there may be times when your child is not getting the proper resources or attention they need to maximize their progress. In a situation like this, it is up to you to advocate for what your child needs. First and foremost, remember that you have all the power as a parent and are inherently your child's best advocate. Having to fight for your child's rights can be intimidating, but the level of passion and dedication you bring will ensure that you will always see what's in your child's best interest and fight for them to get it. As I stressed earlier, you know your child better than anyone else, and you have the power to make educational decisions that are the best and most appropriate for them.

The first step in becoming an effective advocate is to stay informed. Make sure you're familiar with your child's rights and your rights as a parent. Have copies of all past and current evaluation reports, and make sure you fully understand your child's program and whatever accommodations are currently being made to meet their needs. Always ask for additional evaluations and clarification when you feel you need it. There's no such thing as a stupid question; questions will always increase your knowledge and expertise, so don't be afraid to ask them.

Plan and prepare by building relationships with your child's teachers and trainers, educate yourself on how special education programs are managed in your school district, and keep all of your child's records in an organized file. If your child has a 504 plan or Individualized Education Program (IEP) (guidelines the school has agreed to follow to best support your child), consider creating a 504/IEP binder to keep all of your child's goals, progress reports, and assessments in a central location.

If you don't agree with the services your child is getting, don't be afraid to speak up. You won't see the changes you want unless you actively and repeatedly ask for them. Remember that even the best-intentioned teachers and trainers have many other kids competing for their attention and time, so if you want them to prioritize your child, you may have to ask them to do so. Attend meetings with a list of problems you've identified and some solutions you would like to propose. To advocate is to negotiate—this means you not only are highlighting what is wrong about the current system, but also are prepared with realistic alternatives for the team to discuss.

Many school districts offer parent special education committee meetings, where caregivers can share and learn from other parents who have experience advocating for their children's needs. There are also groups on social media specifically designed to give parents the space to learn how to better navigate the school system and obtain the resources their children need.

Last, don't ever feel pressured or rushed to make a decision concerning the best course of action for your child. You have the time and the freedom to make the choice you are most comfortable with. If you do not feel completely content with a decision, do not agree to it; another meeting will be called to address your needs. When you are satisfied, sign the new IEP or 504 plan. No matter what you are told or encouraged to do, know that taking your time is okay. Slow, steady, and determined wins the race.

COORDINATING CAREGIVERS: YOU ARE THE HUB

You have the privilege of being able to track your child's progress across multiple settings and different professional services. This central position in your child's life also allows you to be a "home base" for caregivers and trainers and make sure everyone is collaborating with one another effectively.

As mentioned earlier, it's very likely that each trainer will have a different focus for their time with your child, but that does not mean they can't work on skills that complement each other across different areas of life. Although different fields have specific approaches or guidelines for their practice, working from a multidisciplinary approach ensures that all necessary skills will be addressed. For instance, an occupational therapist may be working with your child on how to carefully trace a letter. A speech therapist might complement this goal by having your child say each letter aloud as it is traced. You may contribute by implementing a reinforcement procedure in which a reinforcer is delivered during each appropriate instance of tracing and saying the letter. In this way, all trainers have worked together to teach a new skill within their individual scopes of practice.

Effective collaboration among professionals means there is a greater chance that more goals will be achieved in a shorter amount of time, because everyone is working cohesively toward similar outcomes. One way to encourage trainers to work together is to schedule a group meeting where all professionals can come together to discuss their current goals and strategies, creating a space where trainers are motivated to work together for the greater good of your child. If an in-person meeting just isn't feasible, suggest a conference call or Skype meeting. If professionals work together in a productive and constructive way, your child's increases in skills and decreases in maladaptive behavior will be consistent across all settings, time, and people.

Encourage your child's trainers to update you regularly on the progress your child is making so you can share this news with other trainers. If you feel comfortable doing so, you can create a confidential group where all trainers and caregivers can frequently update one another on mastered targets, new goals, potential reinforcers, and changes to the programs. You can give consent for other trainers to access one another's progress notes so all parties remain consistent in goal setting and intervention approach.

Because you likely spend more time with your child than anyone else, you also serve as the community coach and create numerous opportunities for your child to practice skills by recruiting others to get involved and implementing certain strategies carefully and accurately. For example, if your child is learning to count money and identify certain bills, you may take them to a store and walk them through how to make a purchase using the right amount of money and counting their change. Now, you have just created a natural opportunity for your child to practice a learned skill in a new setting with novel people.

You are the epicenter of your child's success. By harnessing these powerful ABA tools and sharing them with others who work with your child, you not only increase your child's opportunities for reinforced learning, but also equip these trainers to enact positive changes in the lives of other people they come in contact with. ABA is the gift that keeps on giving!

CHAPTER TEN

A Bright Future

ABA: A HIGHLY ADAPTABLE STRATEGY

ABA is a therapeutic intervention that has helped improve the lives of people with special needs for decades. One of the many reasons ABA has remained the gold standard for autism treatment is because it is as individualized as the people it serves. The principles of behavior upon which ABA relies are applicable to nearly every situation. ABA is used in classrooms, treatment centers, child-care agencies, and sports facilities, to name a few situations in which this powerful training method is helping people meet their goals.

Although ABA is not an autism-specific intervention, the flexibility and adaptability of its application have solidified its position as a successful, life-changing behavioral strategy. When ABA is customized to the needs of the individual and is implemented mindfully, it's sure to result in effective—often amazing—behavior change.

ABA can be implemented in many different ways, such as in play-based environments, structured classroom settings, at home in individual settings, or even within social group activities. Regardless of the purpose or setting, ABA has established itself as an effective, evidence-based tool for positive behavior change. With the work you've been doing with your child, you are becoming a knowledgeable and mindful implementer of ABA strategies.

Learn the ABCs of Any Situation

The ABCs of ABA are the building blocks of any behavior change program. The previous chapters laid the groundwork for your new intervention and gave you the tools to teach new skills to and shape positive behavior in your child. The ABCs, however, also help you identify what is maintaining any existing unwanted behavior and decide what you can do about it.

As you learned in chapter 2, *A* is the antecedent, the event that happens before the behavior takes place; *B* is the behavior, the response the person engages in after the antecedent takes place; and *C* is the consequence, anything that follows the behavior and determines its future frequency. The only way to learn the ABCs of any situation is to observe and report. At times, a behavior can happen so quickly that you do not even realize what preceded it or you deliver a consequence so quickly that it may not be, in retrospect, what you intended to say or do.

Learning the ABCs means taking each situation one step at a time and carefully determining the antecedent, which will give you clues about the behavior's function (e.g., attention, access, escape). You start by noting the behavior that's occurring. The best way to do this is by recording the behavior on the ABC data sheet you created in chapter 2 (page 13).

After you record the behavior, brainstorm what immediately preceded it and record that under the antecedent section. Once you know the antecedent to the behavior, you can more accurately decipher the behavior's function and deliver a consequence to match your desired outcome for the same behavior in the future.

The more you practice identifying the ABCs in each situation, the faster you'll be able to respond effectively to your child's behavior any time, anywhere. Now that you know how to use reinforcement, punishment, extinction, and differential reinforcement procedures, you have multiple tools at your fingertips to choose from to help create and shape positive behavior.

Creating Action Plans

The previous chapters equipped you with the knowledge and tools necessary to create your own ABA curriculum that best suits the needs of your child and family. You have learned the power of reinforcement and the effects of punishment, as well as how to use each to achieve a desired outcome in the same way an ABA professional would. Despite the breadth and depth of your ABA knowledge or how well organized your new intervention is, they are not going to effect change without a well-designed action plan.

Each previous chapter has outlined an action plan specific to the principle you learned. The ultimate goal, however, is for you to create an action plan for any desired behavior or strategy you choose to use. With that said, certain fundamental components should be included in your action plan, regardless of the desired outcome for the behavior.

The first part of any action plan is identifying the behavior you are seeking to change, ensuring that it is clearly defined and is a target that can be easily observed and measured. The behavior's definition should be so clearly stated that anyone who reads it can understand it perfectly. In addition to having this clarity, your behavior change plan should be outlined step by step, and the goal for the behavior should be clearly stated so you and others know when mastery has been obtained.

The next part is the baseline. This is where you collect your ABC data and record the rate, frequency, intensity, or duration of the behavior *before* you begin implementing your intervention. Once you start your intervention, you cannot determine whether it is truly effective unless you know where the behavior was before you started. Your baseline data help you observe progress or signals when you need to change your approach because what you are doing is not effective. Let's say your child was having 20 tantrums per week, and your behavior reduction strategy resulted in a permanent increase in the frequency of tantrums over time. In that case, you know your approach is not working. However, if you did not collect baseline data, you might assume your intervention is working, even if the number of tantrums increased, because you had nothing to compare it to.

Your action plan should also include clear information on how to record, calculate, and interpret the data you collect.

By clearly outlining your action plan, you can help ensure the success of your behavior change program and simplify its use for yourself and anyone else who plays an active role in the intervention process.

REINFORCING OLD SKILLS AND LEARNING NEW ONES

The purpose of ABA, in general, is to make significant changes to help improve our lives and the lives of people we love or care for. For you, that may mean teaching your child how to clean their own body or tie their own shoes. Maybe it means showing your child alternative ways to ask for things they want, instead of crying or yelling. When your child has achieved a goal, you will probably want to take a sigh of relief and celebrate—you *do* deserve to celebrate your child's progress. However, remember that behavior change does not stop there. It is just as important to reinforce old skills as it is to reinforce those your child is currently learning.

Remember, any behavior you want to see more of should be reinforced. Once your child has mastered something, you may be tempted to sit back and tell yourself that they've got it and can move on. Unfortunately, this can cause your child's behavior to backtrack, and they may once again need prompting for a previously mastered behavior. This is why you must be mindful to continuing reinforcing all your child's old acquired skills, even as you are introducing new ones.

Imagine if your boss stopped offering you a monthly bonus (positive reinforcement) when you go above and beyond at work, because you have been doing it for so long that you don't seem to need reinforcement for it anymore. Chances are that your desire to go above and beyond would not last very long, because there is no longer an incentive to continue pushing forward. Similarly, your child needs to know that the positive behavior changes they have made are still important, even though time has passed since they mastered them. Although their positive behavior may not receive as much reinforcement as it did before, the fact that it continues to be recognized will ensure that its frequency remains high.

As you continue to set new goals for your child, you will learn new and creative ways to deliver reinforcers. For example, I once taught a client to tie his shoes independently. Although we had moved on to new behavior goals, he was so proud of his ability to tie his shoes that we used shoe tying as a reinforcer for the new behaviors. Whenever he would get an answer from his new behavior goal right, he wanted to spend a break practicing how to tie his "big" shoe. This provided a built-in opportunity for me to reinforce his shoe-tying behavior while reinforcing the new behaviors. This scenario is not the norm, but as long as you are taking the time to reinforce both old and new behaviors, your behavior change plan will continue to succeed.

SEEKING SPECIALIZED CARE

The concepts in this book are easy to implement in your home and are effective in creating monumental positive behavior change. Now that you have learned and implemented them, you are in a position to create a treatment plan that best fits your child. These tools will allow you to select target behaviors you want to teach and increase through reinforcement and identify problem behaviors you want to reduce through the careful use of punishment or extinction. In addition to your newly created ABA plan, I encourage you to seek out additional resources in your area, if available, that can supplement the principles you've learned in this book and further promote positive behavior change in your child's life.

People with autism are as unique and complex as each of their strengths and weaknesses. Therefore, I recommend that you consider a wide array of supportive services for your child. These supportive services will only enhance the changes you have already made and will further increase your child's probability of success and acquisition of independent living skills. Each professional comes from a very distinct treatment approach and aims to improve a specific need within their shared client. As mentioned in chapter 9, it's a great benefit to your child to have a team of specialized professionals willing to collaborate with one another effectively to reach common goals in a cohesive and organized manner.

Psychologists and BCBAs

When a parent suspects their child has autism, they will likely take the child to be evaluated by a psychologist trained in assessment to help them determine if their child meets the criteria for an autism diagnosis. If your child has already been diagnosed or if you suspect your child may have autism, you have probably already been in contact with a psychologist or perhaps a BCBA. Or maybe you are already receiving services from these professionals.

Psychologists and BCBAs often work together to create a comprehensive behavioral plan for the treatment of people with autism. Although an individual can be both a psychologist and a BCBA, this is not always the case. A psychologist is a doctoral-level mental health provider who has completed 3,000 hours of supervised training and is qualified to administer diagnostic assessments (everyone diagnosed with autism has completed these assessments), conduct individual and group therapy, and collaborate with other health professionals. A BCBA is an individual who has completed a graduate-level degree (either master's or doctorate) in ABA and acquired a minimum of 1,500 hours of supervised behavior-analytic training.

Because BCBAs are behaviorally trained professionals, they are the professionals who most frequently conduct FBAs, create skill acquisition plans, and also create and support the implementation of behavior reduction plans. A BCBA cannot diagnose an individual with any disorder, unless that BCBA is also a licensed psychologist. BCBAs can, however, administer assessments that are behavioral in nature, such as the VB-MAPP, the ABLLS-R, and the AFLS, all of which are behavioral assessments used to evaluate the abilities and needs of individuals with autism.

Other Specialists

In addition to BCBAs and psychologists, many other professionals are trained to work with people with autism and can also evoke positive behavior changes in your child's life. Some of these professionals include speech pathologists, occupational therapists, physical therapists, and social skills coaches.

A speech pathologist is an individual who has completed graduate-level courses in speech and communication disorders and who focuses on assessing, diagnosing, and treating various speech disorders. The overarching goal of a speech pathologist is to ensure that their client can produce speech correctly and understands language and communication. Both occupational and physical therapists work on one's ability to move effectively. The training of occupational therapists, however, focuses on one's ability to complete fine motor actions, while physical therapists work more intensely on the completion of gross motor actions.

Having each of these specialists work collaboratively for one person's benefit is amazing, because each specialist can offer a different perspective and supportive approach. For instance, let's say you have a BCBA working on getting your child to vocally label everything they see. If they are having difficulty achieving this goal, the BCBA may contact your child's speech pathologist to discuss accommodations that would help your child label items more successfully. Conversely, if your child's speech therapist is having difficulty working on particular skills because your child can't remain focused, the BCBA can offer simple suggestions that could motivate your child to participate.

Specialized Facilities

There are many specialized facilities throughout the world with the sole purpose of supporting families with special needs. For example, one such facility with multiple locations in California is the Regional Center, a nonprofit organization focused on giving families access to a plethora of services at little to no cost. Families can go to the Regional Center for free diagnostic testing, evaluations and referrals for supportive services, and even funding for ABA and other therapies that may be impossible for them to afford otherwise. Each client is assigned a case manager who is responsible for helping the family develop a therapeutic plan of action and connecting them with agencies and services that can assist them and help pay for necessary services so the child can get the focus and attention they need regardless of income.

Other specialized facilities include nonpublic agencies or schools geared specifically toward people with special needs. For instance, the Help Group in Los Angeles, California, is a nonprofit organization in charge of more than 10 specialized day schools, special education residential programs, mental and behavioral therapy services, and vocational outreach programs—all of which are geared primarily toward individuals with autism and similar diagnoses. The Help Group's dedication to the special needs community means that they get to provide support to more than 6,000 special needs children throughout California.

Although specialized facilities like these are not available in all locations, they serve as a symbol of what constant dedication and compassion can achieve. Research specialized facilities in your state to find out what might be available to you and your child.

Support Groups: Online and In-Person

Living with and caring for a child with autism can be quite overwhelming and even, at times, discouraging, especially if you are one of the few parents in your area with a special needs child. It can be easy for parents to feel alone or misunderstood, especially if they are not surrounded by others with firsthand experience in similar circumstances.

Support groups are essential for parental self-care and support. They give parents and other caregivers an opportunity to share information with regard to special education policy changes, new community programs that support children with special needs, and even different products that may help simplify some portion of their lives. It also gives parents the time and space to share their frustrations and feel supported and validated by others.

With the mounting list of responsibilities that special needs parents have to tend to, it may be difficult to attend in-person support groups. Fortunately, a plethora of support groups specifically geared toward caregivers of people with autism is available online across different social media platforms. These online support groups make it easier to connect with other parents, because it can be done on their own time and does not require travel. It also allows parents to resonate with people all around the world who share similar experiences. The availability of these social supports can help you feel a sense of relief and renewed commitment to your unique responsibilities as a special needs parent.

ABA in Action: Nelson's Story

I consider Nelson the ABA poster child for success. When I first met Nelson, he was a nonverbal six-year-old in first grade who desperately struggled to make friends in his social skills group and have his needs met, due to his inability to speak.

When we first started working with him at my clinic, we held sessions for upward of 30 hours per week (he was homeschooled, which made this possible). Because Nelson was nonverbal, the majority of his communication happened through problem behavior. Whenever Nelson was hungry, he would let his parents know by either crying or whining. Our first goal was to work with Nelson to find a more functional mode of communication. Due to his lack of language, our focus was initially on encouraging Nelson to echo the vocal sounds we were making. We worked through each sound in the alphabet, reinforcing each time he correctly copied the sound he heard.

After about two months, Nelson had mastered his ability to vocally imitate sounds he heard. Our next step was to begin turning these simple letter sounds into meaningful speech so he could vocalize what he needed. Rather than his parents responding to his tantrum, they would wait and we would begin by having Nelson touch the item he wanted. Then, we would hold the selected item up and label it for Nelson to imitate.

Because Nelson still did not have adequate speech skills, we focused on shaping the sounds he could make into words. We started by delivering social praise for anything he said when we asked him to label the item. For instance, if he wanted chips, we would hold them up to him and say, "chips." In turn, Nelson would reply with a simple letter sound, such as a hard "c," which we then would reinforce as we delivered the chips. Over time, Nelson's hard "c" turned into "ch," which would then receive even more reinforcement.

Our ability to shape Nelson's language by using items that motivated him helped us progress very quickly. Although we were avidly working on his language skills, he continued to engage in problem behavior, because it had been his primary way to get his needs met for so long. We continued to reinforce Nelson's approximation of each word and also began putting previous problem behaviors on extinction to reduce the frequency of his tantrums. For instance, when Nelson would engage in a tantrum, we would let him know that to get the snack he wanted, he would have to calm down and ask nicely. Needless to say, we encountered an extinction burst that lasted for about three weeks. As we continued to place his tantrum behavior on extinction, we increased our schedule of reinforcement when he asked for things appropriately—a combination you now know to be differential reinforcement.

The more we continued reinforcing Nelson's behavior by giving him the treat and telling him how proud we were, the more he started asking for things appropriately, and the less his tantrums seemed to happen. To make sure Nelson was generalizing these skills across settings and people, I trained Nelson's babysitter to implement the same DRO schedule so he could practice and maintain his skills with her—and it worked! His parents even let us know that he had begun to ask for toys nicely with the other children in his social skills group.

Within a year and a half of our first session, Nelson seemed like a different child. He basked in all the attention and social praise he received from adults when he used his words, and it seemed as if he were always talking. I am confident his improved speech and increased self-confidence also translated to his social interactions with peers, because he started making friends with some of the children his age within the group.

Ultimately, I had to stop working with Nelson, because he and his parents relocated. But sometime after their departure, I received an e-mail from his parents letting me know that Nelson had been given a school award for being "most friendly" and was thriving in third grade. Experiences like these constantly remind me of how life-changing the use of ABA can be, and how important it is to remain consistent and focused on the goal.

ONWARD AND UPWARD!

You have come quite a long way since chapter 1. You have learned an incredible amount of information about ABA, and I am confident this information will equip you with the fundamental skills you need to create effective behavior change programs for your child. You learned about different types of reinforcement and punishment, the power of extinction, and the importance of induction and generalization, as well as how to teach complex behaviors.

You are now in a position to better understand the functions behind your child's problem behaviors, and you are more knowledgeable about your child's individual needs and their ability to communicate them. You also know how to teach your child more effective modes of communication that can replace some of their undesirable behaviors. By teaching them key adaptive and social skills, you are setting your child up for a future of success, greater independence, and meaningful connection with others. Although you have reached the end of this book, this is only the start of your ABA journey.

The process of learning and the application of knowledge are lifelong pursuits. As your child continues to grow, so will you and your ability to assess and meet their needs. The techniques used in ABA are timeless and will always be applicable to your child, whatever the situation. The task will be for you to decide when and how you will do the work. Refer back to these techniques and the examples presented throughout this book as a guide for navigating your child's behavior. If you continue to implement these skills in your child's life, as well as in your own, no matter the circumstance, you will continue to be amazed by your potential for success. And so, onward and upward! This is only the beginning, the first step on the path to your child's bright future.

GLOSSARY

antecedent: The event or stimulus that occurs right before a behavior

applied behavior analysis (ABA): A science centered on strengthening positive, socially adaptive behavior by making changes to a person's immediate environment

backward chaining: A chaining procedure in which an individual is taught a behavior starting with the final step and then, through mastery of each step, progresses to the first step until all steps can be done independently

behavior: Anything a person says or does; also known as response

behavioral contrast: When, in a specific environment, a behavior changes in the opposite direction than it does in the environment where punishment is being implemented

complex behavior: Large behaviors that are made up of a chain of smaller behaviors

consequence: The event that occurs after the behavior and determines if the behavior will increase or decrease in the future

corporal punishment: A type of positive punishment (with "positive" meaning the *addition* of something); the delivery of physical pain in response to an undesirable behavior

differential reinforcement: A procedure that involves the combination of reinforcement and extinction to increase desired behavior and reduce unwanted or problematic behavior

differential reinforcement of other behaviors (DRO): When reinforcement is delivered contingent on the absence of a specific problem behavior and the problem behavior is placed on extinction; see *differential reinforcement, extinction*

extinction: The act of no longer reinforcing a behavior that used to receive reinforcement; also known as a nonevent

extinction burst: The temporary increase in frequency, intensity, or duration of a behavior when an extinction procedure is initially introduced; typically referred to as the "it gets worse before it gets better" phenomenon

fading: Gradual removal of applied prompts, resulting in the independent completion of the behavioral goal

flexibility: Ability to "go with the flow" within both conversation and routine; ability to cope amidst unforeseen change

forward chaining: A chaining procedure in which an individual starts at the very beginning of a chain of behaviors and does not move on to the next step until the previous step is mastered

functional behavior assessment (FBA): An analytical process based on observation, which helps determine the function of behavior, brainstorm ways in which function can be met more appropriately, and determine what changes can be made in the environment to better support the behavior change

generalization: When a response taught in one setting and under one set of circumstances is emitted in similar settings and environments without prior teaching

induction: When variations of a taught behavior appear in the presence of the original stimulus or antecedent without prior teaching

interval: A schedule of reinforcement; refers to a predetermined passage of time

least-to-most prompting: When the smallest and least intrusive prompt is used before attempting to use a more intrusive prompt

most-to-least prompting: When the largest and most intrusive prompt is used and then systematically reduced

negative reinforcement: A consequence wherein something undesired or negative is removed after a behavior, which results in an increase in that behavior in the future

negative punishment: A consequence wherein something desired or positive is removed after a behavior, which results in a decrease in that behavior in the future

overcorrection: A type of positive punishment; restoring the environment to a condition that is better than when you started the undesirable behavior

positive practice: A type of positive punishment; repeatedly engaging in an appropriate replacement for the undesirable behavior, either for a certain number of times or for a specific duration

positive punishment: A consequence wherein something undesired or negative is added or delivered after a behavior, which results in a decrease in that behavior in the future

positive reinforcement: A consequence wherein something desired or positive is added or delivered after a behavior, which results in an increase in that behavior in the future

prompt: A temporary supportive stimulus that helps an individual emit a response

prompt dependence: When one will not start or complete an activity without a prompt, even if they know how to do it

punishment: The addition or removal of something that leads to a decrease in behavior; see *positive punishment, negative punishment*

ratio: A schedule of reinforcement; refers to a certain number of responses

reinforcement: The addition or removal of something that leads to an increase in behavior; see *positive reinforcement, negative reinforcement*

reinforcer: Anything that comes after the occurrence of a behavior and increases the likelihood the behavior will happen again in the future

response blocking: A type of positive punishment; to physically prevent someone from engaging in an undesirable behavior

response cost: The loss of a certain amount of a reinforcer caused by engaging in a certain behavior

schedule of reinforcement: A method used to determine the frequency and timing of the reinforcer being delivered

shaping: Differential reinforcement of successive approximations toward a target behavior

socioemotional reciprocity: One's ability to engage in "normal" social interactions, such as conversation, expression of emotion, and the sharing of common interests

spontaneous recovery: When a previously extinguished behavior temporarily reappears after some time

stimulus generalization: The tendency to respond in new settings and around new people the same way as in situations with familiar people and settings

time-out: A temporary form of physical isolation that causes the child to lose access to natural reinforcers like talking to friends or eating dinner with family

total task presentation: A chaining procedure in which every step in a behavior chain is taught each time the complex behavior is presented

verbal reprimand: A type of positive punishment; a verbal warning used to express disappointment or disapproval

ADDITIONAL RESOURCES

Autism NOW

A national source for community-based solutions that provides resources for those with autism, their family members, professionals in the field, and caregivers.

- www.autismnow.org
- 855-828-8476

The Autism Society of America

This organization hosts the most comprehensive national autism conference and is the front-runner in the fight for policy change for individuals with disabilities and special education needs.

- www.autism-society.org
- 800-328-8476

Autism Speaks

Autism Speaks connects families with services in their community, hosts various support groups, and holds one of the largest national annual fundraisers for autism.

- www.autismspeaks.org
- 888-288-4762

Autism Support from the US Department of Health and Human Services

General information, screening and diagnosis, treatment and research, and a list of other organizations involved with autism.

- www.hhs.gov/programs/topic-sites/autism/index.html
- 877-696-6775

Autism Support Network

This support group offers an online support community, a list of resources for further learning, and news and events.

- www.autismsupportnetwork.com
- 203-404-4929

The Help Group

A nonprofit organization based in California with more than 10 specialized day schools, special education residential programs, mental and behavioral therapy services, and vocational outreach programs—all of which are geared primarily toward individuals with autism and similar diagnoses.

- www.thehelpgroup.org
- 877-994-3588

LA FEAT

This nonprofit organization based in Los Angeles provides guidance and hosts support groups for parents of children newly diagnosed with autism. They often host professionals within the autism community to share valuable information with attendees.

- www.lafeat.org
- E-mail: michael@lafeat.org

L.A. Parent

L.A. Parent is dedicated to creating a space where parents of children with all abilities can feel supported. They host multiple free special needs resource fairs throughout the year to give parents an opportunity to connect with services available in their area. They also distribute one of the most far-reaching special needs resource magazines in southern California.

- www.laparent.com
- 818-264-2222

REFERENCES

Dawson, G., E. J. H. Jones, K. Merkle, K. Venema, R. Lowy, S. Faja, D. Kamara, M. Murias, J. Greenson, J. Winter, M. Smith, S. J. Rogers, and S. J. Webb. "Early Behavioral Intervention Is Associated with Normalized Brain Activity in Young Children with Autism." *Journal of the American Academy of Child and Adolescent Psychiatry* 51, no. 11 (2012): 1150–9. doi:10.1016/j.jaac.2012.08.018.

Luby, J., A. Belden, M. P. Harms, R. Tillman, and D. M. Barch. "Preschool is a Sensitive Period for the Influence of Maternal Support on the Trajectory of Hippocampal Development." *Proceedings of the National Academy of Sciences: Early Edition* 113, no. 20 (2016): 5742–47. doi:10.1073/pnas.1601443113.

Strassberg, Z., K. A. Dodge, G. S. Pettit, and J. E. Bates. "Spanking in the Home and Children's Subsequent Aggression toward Kindergarten Peers." *Development and Psychopathology* 6, no. 3 (1994): 445–61. doi.org/10.1017/S0954579400006040.

APPENDIX: BLANK DATA SHEETS

ABC Data Sheet

TIME	ANTECEDENT	BEHAVIOR	CONSEQUENCE	POSSIBLE FUNCTION (OR PURPOSE)

Reinforcement Data Sheet

DATE	TIME	TARGET BEHAVIOR	REINFORCER USED	RESULTS (+ OR -)

Response Cost Data Sheet

INTERVAL #	NUMBER OF _____ LEFT	RESULTS (+ OR -)
1		
2		
3		
4		
5		
6		
7		
8		
9		
10		

Frequency Extinction Data Sheet

For _____ (target behavior)

Behavior Goal: _____

DAYS	FREQUENCY OF PROBLEM BEHAVIOR
Baseline 1	
Baseline 2	
Baseline 3	
Extinction Day 1	
Extinction Day 2	
Extinction Day 3	

Duration Extinction Data Sheet

For _____ (target behavior)

Behavior Goal: _____

DAYS	DURATION OF PROBLEM BEHAVIOR (MINUTES)
Baseline 1	
Baseline 2	
Baseline 3	
Extinction Day 1	
Extinction Day 2	
Extinction Day 3	

DRO Data Sheet

Interval Time: _____

Problem Behavior: _____

INTERVAL NUMBER	NUMBER OF OCCURRENCES	RESULTS (+ OR −)
1		
2		
3		
4		
5		
6		
7		
8		
9		
10		

Complex Behavior Data Sheet

Target Behavior:_____

DATE	STEPS TO BE COMPLETED	COMPLETED INDEPENDENTLY (+ OR −)

Social Skills Data Sheet

SOCIAL SKILLS GOAL	LOCATIONS TARGETED	NUMBER OF INDIVIDUALS	COMPLETED INDEPENDENTLY (+ OR –)

INDEX

A

Access function, extinction
protocols for, 50
Accidental reinforcement, 21,
23, 47, 58
Action plans
for chaining, 73
creating action plans, 102–103
differential
reinforcement, 50–51
DRO, 57, 62
for extinction, 50
punishment, 40
reinforcement, 26, 28–29
for social skill
development, 87, 90
Antecedents
ABCs, as an element of, 12, 101
of concerning behavior, 18
defining, 113
induction in the presence of an
antecedent, 116
in negative reinforcement, 24
in sample ABC data
sheets, 13, 120
Applied Behavior Analysis (ABA)
ABCs of, 12–13, 101
in action plans, 87, 102–103

adaptability of
strategy, 17, 100–101
BCBA training in, 105
beginning the process, 5–7
benefits of, 4–5, 8
defining, 3, 113
in Dwayne's Story, 60–61
extinction as a preferred method
of intervention, 45
FBA use, 11
funding assistance, 106
in Hannah's Story, 14–15
intervention strategy
plans, 72–73
in Jayden's Story, 88–89
in Mason's Story, 38–39
negative reinforcement
and, 22, 32
in Nelson's Story, 108–109
nonverbal information,
decoding, 10
parental role in treatment
process, 17–18, 99
positive punishments, types
of, 32–33
social skills, applied to, 80
teachers, sharing ABA techniques
with, 95–96

Attention function, extinction
protocols for, 51

B
Backward chaining, 66, 67, 78, 113
Behavior *See also* Applied behavior
analysis; Complex behavior
ABCs, as an element of, 12, 101
behavior goals in action
plans, 40, 41
behavioral contrast, 36–37, 113
behaviorism, 3
ignoring inappropriate
behavior, 15, 44, 45, 48,
51, 55, 61
maladaptive behavior, 3, 11, 21,
23–24, 27, 94, 96, 99
sample data sheets, charting
target behaviors in, 13, 30, 121
Board Certified Behavior Analysis
(BCBA), 2, 104–105, 106
Bribery *vs.* reinforcement, 25–26

C
Chaining
in action plan, 73
backward chaining, 66, 67, 78, 113
for conversation practice, 80
forward chaining, 66, 67, 78, 114
shaping, confusing with, 69–70
Complex behaviors
action plan steps, 76–77, 87
defining, 65, 113
methods of teaching, 66–67,
67–68, 80–81
sample complex behavior data
sheets, 77, 126

total task presentation, as
part of, 116
Consequences
ABCs, as an element of, 12, 101
in action plans, 40, 41
defining, 113
in Hannah's Story, 14
negative consequences of
punishment, 56
in negative reinforcement, 22–23,
24, 25, 114
in positive reinforcement, 115
punishment and, 31–32
reinforcers as types of, 12, 19
in sample ABC data
sheets, 13, 120
Corporal punishment, 33, 113
Crossing the street, steps in
behavior chain, 67–68
Cursing, reducing with extinction
procedure, 48–49

D
Data sheets
blank data sheets, 120
complex behavior
data, 76–77, 126
DRO data, 62, 63, 125
extinction data, 51–53, 123, 124
getting started, 7
ongoing records, importance of
maintaining, 16
reinforcement data, 29, 30, 121
response cost data, 41, 42, 122
social skills data, 90, 91, 127
Differential reinforcement
defining, 54–55, 113

Interval schedule of
reinforcement, 28, 114

J
Jumping on furniture, DRO
procedure to end, 57

M
Marbles, use of in action
plans, 40–42, 63

N
Negative punishment
in action plan, 40
defining, 114
extinction, comparing to, 45
in Mason's Story, 39
positive punishment and, 32, 42
types of, 33–34
Negative reinforcement, 20,
22–24, 25, 30, 37, 114
Nonverbal communication, 9–10,
85, 89, 108

O
Organizational behavior
management (OBM), 5
Overcorrection, 33, 115

P
Parent-child relationship,
punishment affecting, 35,
42, 45–46
Positive behaviors
ABA as an effective strategy,
6, 100–101

in action plans, 18, 58–59
continued recognition for, 103
differential reinforcement
and, 54, 56–57, 64
specialists assisting
with, 104–107
teacher involvement, 95–96
Positive language, 26
Positive practice, 33, 115
Positive punishment
in action plan, 40
corporal punishment as a
type of, 113
defining, 115
examples of, 45
in Mason's Story, 39
types of, 32–33
verbal reprimands, 116
Positive reinforcement
in action plans, 26, 28–29
continued recognition for, 103
defining, 30, 115
in Ella's Story, 27
examples of, 24–25
negative *vs.*, 20–22
Prompting
in action plans, 40, 73
least-to-most
prompting, 71, 76, 114
most-to-least prompting, 70,
73, 74, 114
for previously mastered
behavior, 103
prompt dependency, 16, 71,
76, 78, 115
in sample complex behavior data
sheet, 77

with teens, 80
See also Fading prompts
Prosocial behavior, 4, 27, 34–35, 58, 87, 91
Punishment. *See also* Negative punishment; Positive punishment
in action plans, 40, 41, 42, 104
behavioral contrast and, 113
consequences, associating with, 12
defining, 32–34, 115
differential reinforcement as an alternative to, 55–57
extinction as an alternative to, 43–46, 53
learning under punishment conditions, 25
in Mason's Story, 38–39
negative reinforcement and, 22, 23
reinforcement *vs.*, 34–36
sparing use of, 37–38, 42
types of, 33

R

Ratio schedule of reinforcement, 28, 115
Reinforcers
action plan, steps in implementing, 41
in action plan, 40
as changing over time, 6, 28
consequences as reinforcers, 12, 19
consistent use of, 24
coordination in implementing, 98, 99
creative delivery of, 103–104
defining, 19, 115
DRO and delivery of, 57–58, 59
in Ella's Story, 27
extinction, discovering unwanted reinforcers through, 43
highly preferred reinforcers, 83
home, continuing training at, 93–94, 95
in Mason's Story, 39
in reinforcement data sheets, 30, 121
response cost as loss of reinforcers, 34
social praise, 84
timing of delivery, 25, 28
in token system, 28–29
weak reinforcers, 23
See also Negative reinforcement; Positive reinforcement
Response blocking, 33, 115
Response cost, 34, 39, 40, 115
Response cost data sheets, 42, 122

S

Shaping, 68–70, 73, 78, 108, 115
Siblings and differential reinforcement, 57
Skinner, B. F., 3. See also *Behaviorism*
Social skills
in action plans, 87, 90, 91
conversational skills, improving, 82–83
empathy, teaching, 85–86
induction and generalization, problems with, 80–81
in Jayden's Story, 88–89

reciprocity, 84–85

specific targets, focus on, 79–80

Socioemotional reciprocity, 84, 115

Specialized care options, 104–107

Speech regression in Ella's
Story, 27

Spontaneous recovery, 47,
49, 50, 116

Stimulus generalization, 81, 116

T

Tantrums

baseline data, collecting, 11, 102

bribery, short-term use of, 26

escaping homework through, 24

extinction procedure as response
to, 44, 50

in Nelson's Story, 108–109

punishment and, 45

unintentional
reinforcement of, 47

Teachers, 21, 34, 47, 95–96, 97

Teens, overcoming conversation
challenges, 80, 83, 86, 87–90

Text messages, teaching
appropriate frequency
of, 82–83

Time-out, 34

Total task presentation, 67, 73, 78

V

Verbal reprimands, 33, 88, 116

W

Watson, John, 3

ABOUT THE AUTHOR

Victoria M. Boone, MA, is a Board Certified Behavior Analyst (BCBA) and behavior change consultant. She is the founder and clinical director of The Hamilton Center in Van Nuys, California, an ABA agency dedicated to helping individuals improve the quality of their lives, one day at a time. In her spare time, she supervises graduate students passionate about ABA, trains staff on the implementation of various techniques, and hosts parent education seminars and professional workshops in the community.